WHEN YOUR
LOVER DIES

WHEN YOUR LOVER DIES

DEALING WITH GRIEF AFTER A SPOUSE'S DEATH

Robert C. Brigham

iUniverse, Inc.
New York   Lincoln   Shanghai

WHEN YOUR LOVER DIES
DEALING WITH GRIEF AFTER A SPOUSE'S DEATH

iUniverse books may be ordered through booksellers or by contacting:

iUniverse
2021 Pine Lake Road, Suite 100
Lincoln, NE 68512
www.iuniverse.com
1-800-Authors (1-800-288-4677)

Because of the dynamic nature of the Internet, any Web addresses or links contained in this book may have changed since publication and may no longer be valid.

The views expressed in this work are solely those of the author and do not necessarily reflect the views of the publisher, and the publisher hereby disclaims any responsibility for them.

ISBN: 978-0-595-48633-5 (pbk)
ISBN: 978-0-595-60727-3 (ebk)

Printed in the United States of America

To my late wife

Deirdre

and to

lovers everywhere

Contents

Acknowledgments

I am indebted to all in my family and circle of friends who have provided support and encouragement for this undertaking, particularly my daughter, Rosalind Brigham Penney, and my special friend, Patricia Ann Madden.

Several trusted individuals agreed to read the manuscript. All tackled the task conscientiously and suggested many significant improvements. They are Meryl Klein Hostetler, Molly Kinnaird Johnston, Monica Gronert Klepp, Gretchen Lotz, Patricia Ann Madden, Rosalind Brigham Penney, and Joseph M. Wier.

There are not enough words to express appreciation to my editor, Diane Sears, whose encouragement, enthusiasm, ideas and editorial skills moved this work from stagnation to completion.

A special tribute is owed my wife, Deirdre Davis Brigham, for showing me an incredible life, full of love and excitement—a life that provided the motivation to write this book.

Preface

One way or another, we will part.

Making Friends with Death by Judith L. Lief

This is a book about lovers, and their separation by death. To a large extent it's a personal story, but I hope the words have meaning beyond myself. What I'm talking about here is love—true everlasting love. It doesn't matter if the lovers are married or cohabiting, straight or gay, young or old. Love is love. As my wife said, "Love is too rare and too beautiful not to seize it wherever you find it." So I dedicate these pages to all who have found—and perhaps already lost—their mate.

Over the span of a lifetime, tragedy may visit often or infrequently. You may feel immune to its tentacles for years, even decades. Then, suddenly, your gut will be wrenched by lost employment, demolished home, or deteriorating health. Even if the fates spare you such calamities, eventually, in one form or another, you must deal with the heartbreak of death. How you handle it can color the rest of your life.

Each death, each grief, and each response is unique. These pages deal only with the specific tragedy of the loss of a lover. They make no attempt to discuss the myriad other disasters that can strike. And, even in this restricted area, two individuals' situations can differ markedly. For example, my loss occurred in later life, clearly a circumstance far from one that leaves a widow with several small children. Nevertheless, the widow and I share the traumatic death of a spouse, and our individual grieving processes will present similarities.

You have a right to ask, "Who does he think he is, daring to lecture on this personal and painful subject?" After all, I'm not a doctor, therapist, or clergyman. Oh, I may have picked up a bit of knowledge from my counselor wife and by volunteering at a crisis intervention agency. But what truly does justify this work, what more than overcomes any and all other failings, is my wife—my lover—died, leaving me devastated, helpless, defeated, sobbing, angry, and vaguely suicidal. I know what it's like. I suppose books by "experts," and even by others who have lost their true love, are helpful. However, I found they all too often didn't speak to me or were too complex at a time when simplicity was what I required. Hopefully this work is different.

This is a tale of survival, a quest that continues to this day. Thus, while this book deals with death, in the final analysis it is about life. Perhaps by reading my story, you'll see some parts of yourself and know you're not alone, that what you're feeling is okay. Perhaps by learning where I wish I'd acted differently, you can avoid some heartbreak. To the extent my words are helpful to others, I am thankful. To the extent they don't apply to another, I am understanding. Each of us is different, and each of us deals with pain in unique ways.

Just a few words about the organization. This book is divided into three major divisions. Part 1 concentrates on life before any death occurs, beginning early in the union. I believe, in retrospect, a person best begins handling a lover's loss by accepting its inevitability while the relationship flourishes. Therefore, the book starts with this concept and advances through the death itself. Then in Part 2 we deal with the immediate and long-term aftermaths. If you were attracted to this book because your lover already has died, I recommend you skip Part 1 and turn directly to Chapter 4. If, on the other hand, separation seems in the distant future, read Chapters 1 through 4, and then place the book on a shelf where, hopefully, it will gather dust for decades. Part 3 presents a brief commentary on where I was seven years after my wife's death, and some advice for dealing with friends who have experienced a loss. Each chapter concludes with a summary of its salient points.

Since any insights I may possess arise from the experience with my wife, I employ "she" or "her" throughout. I hope the reader will replace these with the appropriate pronouns. In the same vein, I use "marriage" and "spouse" to refer to the specific union and individual considered here. Simply substitute the words that apply to you.

I have inserted short vignettes when I felt they were relevant. I created several of these myself, most during the first year after my wife died and a few much later. I include them as examples of my attempt to cope at the time they were written.

As you continue reading, keep in mind that if there is any theme in this effort, it is *whatever works is good!* So take what you like from these pages, and discard the rest. *There is no right way—except for your way.*

PART 1

FROM MARRIAGE TO DEATH

Chapter 1

The Halcyon Days

Wilt thou love her, comfort her, honor and keep her in sickness and in health … so long as ye both shall live?

Wedding ceremony of Robert and Deirdre Brigham, June 22, 1957

I was born in Newark, New Jersey, on September 20, 1934, and raised in adjacent East Orange. Twenty days later, in Orlando, Florida, Deirdre "Dee" Davis announced her presence. For 20 years, our lives would follow separate but parallel courses. We both had slightly flawed and intensely loving parents. My mother was a homemaker and my father an engineer. Dee's parents were educators, her mother a fourth-grade teacher and her father a principal. Both families worked hard and achieved middle-class status.

We were educated in fine public schools. Both of us had typical young lives. I constructed models, played sports (poorly), and as a teen dwelled on girls. Dee studied the violin, water-skied, and as a teen dwelled on boys. Colleges in the Boston area accepted us. Our fate was sealed!

Six weeks shy of my 18th birthday, just a month before I was to leave for college, my 55-year-old father suffered an unexpected and fatal heart attack. This was my first close experience with death. How I wish I knew then what I know now. How my mother must have suffered. I was upset, of course. But I was an egocentric teenager about to leave for college. My mother was a lifelong stoic who typically and courageously donned a brave mask. My life barely changed, and it seemed as if she, too, was doing extremely well. I never imagined the true effect on her—until now.

At college, I studied, partied, and dated. Dee studied, partied, and dated. In the spring of our junior year, on March 19, 1955, we individually agreed to a blind date pushed by mutual friends. Each of us considered canceling, our luck with such friendly assistance having not been the best. Two years, three months, and three days later we wed, both at the age of 22, old for that time but terribly young. And thus began an exciting adventure that twisted and turned through 42 years of a thrill ride that beats any theme park fantasy.

We spent a year in Australia, five more in Orlando, seven in New Jersey, and returned to Orlando to stay in 1970. We produced two thriving children, suffered a miscarriage and a stillborn birth, and constantly worked to learn the elusive skills of parenting and spousing. I wound up teaching mathematics at a state university and volunteering at a crisis intervention/suicide prevention agency. Dee became a therapist, eventually founding and directing a behavioral medicine program for people with life-challenging and life-threatening problems.

Before reaching age 35, Dee contended for the first time with the death of dear ones: a beloved grandmother following a series of strokes, and her mother from an automobile accident. The latter was doubly difficult since Dee had to deal with her father's grief as well as her own. Now I recognize what I observed in him during that period, but at the time, neither of us had any idea of the depths of his torment. I remember saying to Dee, "You know, someday one of us is going to go through what your father is." I said the words, but I didn't believe them. Don't we all think we're going to live forever? One time, while listening to Garrison Keillor on his National Public Radio show *Prairie Home Companion,* I heard him discussing death and, with typical wry humor, saying that each of us is sure a special dispensation will be made to excuse us, and only us, from it. Unfortunately, life (or death) doesn't work that way.

So, accepting at least intellectually that death is a certainty, what can we do, or what should we do at this point in our existence? Not much, really. It would be unnatural, counterproductive, and no fun at all to envisage the scythe-wielding, stern-faced, and black-cloaked reaper trailing us through our daily lives. While many die prematurely young, for the most part we live into our 60s and beyond. Truly death is not imminent and we should not live as if it were.

But if death does come, wouldn't it be better to have treated your mate in a way that minimizes the all-too-natural tendency to say, "if only …" or "why did … bother me so much" or "I could have been a better …"?

If you've ever read an advice columnist (yes, I must admit I did for many years), you've seen such phrases. "My wife always wanted to visit the Grand Canyon, but I was too busy. If only we had." "I hated his snoring. Now I'd give anything to hear it again." "My wife always squeezed the toothpaste in the middle. It drove me crazy." "I loved her, but I never told her." "I could have been more understanding about his work problems."

The list is as long as there are individuals. And no matter who you are, how great a mate you've been, you'll find plenty enough such thoughts popping to mind. The trick is to have lived your life in such a way that you can stop them for a while by saying in all honesty, "But I *was* a good husband. I was kind and gentle and understanding. I made it abundantly clear she was the most important thing in the world to me. I told her every day, several times a day, that I love her, and I backed my words with action."

It would be extremely surprising if you were perfect. After all, it's pretty hard to be, and without a doubt it's annoying as hell to others. Certainly I fell far short. The nice thing is, perfection isn't necessary. By the way, don't expect it in your lover, either.

Consider the above examples, or any others that apply to your life. If you're honest, you'll see the "offenses" are petty. My wife had two basic rules she attempted to follow:

- **Don't sweat the small stuff.**
- **Everything is small stuff.**

These words were later immortalized by Richard Carlson in his book *Don't Sweat the Small Stuff—and it's all small stuff*. I have no argument with the first, but I don't agree completely with the second. There is some "stuff" that is very, very big—like her death. But so much of what bends us out of shape are molehills that assume mountainous proportions only because we construct them ourselves.

It seems clear, then, in these happy and seemingly never-ending early years of your coupled life, that you don't have to do much to prepare for a distant and obviously improbable death. Except, of course, for what you'd do anyway to maximize for both of you the joys of your relationship. Love each other and tell each other. Learn to compromise and to overlook the "small stuff." Redefine most problems as small stuff. Review your marriage or commitment vows and ask yourself why you made them in the first place if you don't intend to keep them. Be supportive and not jealous of your partner's successes. Be supportive and understanding of her failures. Develop a sense of humor. Laugh at each other's jokes (even if they're awful). Talk, talk, talk.

All this does not in any way imply suffocation. Every person needs individual time, goals, and thoughts. You don't have to agree on all matters, just respect the other's views. Physical separations will occur due to work, military obligations, family emergencies, or simply a desire to luxuriate in one's own space. These are all okay and must be supported by the mate. The key is to revel in each other when you have the chance, to maximize those precious, and sadly all-too-short, moments you will have together.

It's really easy—and fun, and the benefits will surpass your most imaginative fantasy.

I read the local paper daily, deriving knowledge from the main section, understanding from the local, nothing from the sports, and wisdom from the comics. Two strips, *Rose is Rose* by Pat Brady and *For Better or for Worse* by Lynn Johnston, are especially appealing. Each draws from the setting of a loving family for its humor. Each, the latter more so, recognizes life doles out problems, including death, that can be handled with love, time, tolerance, understanding, and humor. Surprisingly, there are important messages in these strips.

Somehow Dee and I muddled through these early years, which were filled mostly with joy, but at times presented serious challenges. We emerged with our love intact and strengthened. One day we peeked from our joint cocoon and discovered we were 50!

Key Points from The Halcyon Days

- Love each other at every opportunity.
- Ignore the "small stuff." Convince yourself most problems are small stuff.
- Discuss mistakes, then forgive them and *never* bring them up again.
- Make up soon after arguments.
- Learn to talk with each other.
- Learn to laugh *with* each other (not *at* each other).
- If you have children, raise them with love, recognizing and fostering their individuality. These are admirable goals in any event. And if you remain close to your kids, your later years will be blessed with their friendship and, if necessary, their assistance.

Chapter 2

FACING THE REALITY— THE LATER YEARS

But who is set up for the impossible that is going to happen? Who is set up for tragedy and the incomprehensibility of suffering? Nobody.

American Pastoral by Phillip Roth

No way were we 50! Only others reach such a venerable age. Certainly not us, the youngsters we had always been and still felt we were. Alas, it's just one of many events that happen "only to others," and they begin to occur with ever-increasing frequency. You may have noticed. New pains scornfully snicker—and last longer. You become familiar with doctors whose specialties you didn't know even existed. You run a little slower and, before you realize it, the once routine eight-minute miles have slipped to 10 (or, if you're honest, 11). You tire more easily.

Furthermore, you start thinking about retirement. It's a shock, although not necessarily a bad one. It can be an exciting adventure for you and your mate to plan how to share these precious advanced years. In fact, even the pre-retirement period can be the best of experiences. Children are gone, health is acceptable, and finances are secure. What a great time to revel in each other! If I could pick one period in my life to last forever, it would be this.

Unfortunately, of course, that cannot be. Suddenly, you're well into your 60s, and it becomes increasingly difficult to continue the pretense of immortality. Familiar names, of those your age or younger, appear in the obituaries. Jokes about death don't seem quite as funny. You may already have a will, but now you update it and deal with all those pesky related matters such as durable powers of attorney, living wills, and health care surrogates. You may even consider nursing home insurance, and, when you learn the rates, you'll wish you'd investigated it when you were younger. Remember, you've got to be in good health to get it, so don't wait too long.

Eventually the reality is accepted. We *are* going to die. As one of the comics of the Golden Age of Radio, speaking of death, said, "That's life!" Judith L. Lief's improbably entitled *Making Friends with Death* may prove helpful in reaching this acceptance of the inevitable. It's written from a Buddhist's view, but contains material useful to all.

Hopefully, though, you can escape death for many more years. But it could come soon, and it's best not to ignore the possibility. As in earlier times, this doesn't mean radical changes in lifestyle. In fact, I can think of only two important steps to take at this point. Probably the earlier they are attacked, the better, but it's never too late—except when it really is too late, when one of you is gone.

The first step is easy, even fun if you truly value your relationship. It's the simple principle: Live every day as if it's your last. Well, like so many "simple" concepts, it's harder than it sounds. Now *really* is the time to ignore the small stuff, to reduce the number of arguments, to make up quickly when disagreements do occur, and to tell each other often of your love. I was motivated to follow this path by the image of my father's sudden passing, realizing death could visit me without warning at any time, and I sure didn't want to die in the midst of a fight. Dee never verbally expressed herself regarding this principle, but she certainly lived as though she were a devout believer. Thus the last years of our life together were the best ever, and I think about this whenever guilt attempts its insidious penetration.

The second recommendation I have is not as pleasant. However, by acting on it, you can greatly ease the immediate burden on the surviving mate during a time when decisions must be made and the ability to make them wisely is impaired.

Simply put, you as a couple must discuss your feelings about death and how you want your partner to deal with yours. Probably you'll be in accord on most issues. But if your views differ, it's important to follow the preferences of the deceased on matters that relate to her, no matter how much it may violate your personal taste. If you do, you will have the comfort of knowing your lover received the treatment she desired, and you'll reduce the potential for feeling guilt.

Dee and I had talked some, but not in any detail and not nearly enough. I wish we'd followed my own advice, and the next couple of chapters will indicate the price of failing to do so. I made decisions based on off-the-cuff remarks Dee had uttered over the years, on responses to what she liked and disliked at funerals and memorial services we had attended, and by applying the principle of "what she would want." But I wonder about her true feelings concerning some of the decisions I took.

Furthermore, on the day of her death, I was hit with an unexpected question I answered in a way I wish I hadn't, and it haunts me to this day. I'll get to that later.

It would be easy for someone to say to me, "Well, if your relationship was so great, why didn't you know what to do?" Unfortunately, it doesn't work that way. Being in love does not mean being a mind reader. And this is a time when you don't want to be wrong. So, as always, talk, talk, talk. Together make the decisions that will guide one of you later. Consider not only the subjects mentioned below, but also any others you think relevant.

There are two time frames for you and your mate to discuss: (1) the approach of death and (2) the days, months, and years after.

If you've established living wills, you probably know whether your lover wants to be kept alive by machine and feeding tube, and whether she wants resuscitation if breathing stops. These are heart-rending decisions. While never easy emotionally, it's best if they're previously resolved because then they become justifiable in your mind (and, again, you lose the guilt). We've all read about conflicts between family members on whether to "pull the plug." In most cases, all parties love the affected individual but have different views of what should be done.

Florida and the nation were struck in 2005 with the plight of Terry Schiavo, a young woman who had been in a permanent vegetative state since 1990. Many factors complicated her situation, but simply put, her husband wanted to suspend feeding and her parents were opposed. The legal wrangling was painful for all. I cannot help but wonder if the disagreements would have melted if Terry Schiavo had made her wishes clear—and in writing.

I remember so well being asked on Dee's final morning whether medical staff should attempt to resuscitate her should she stop breathing. I was a wreck, tears streaming down my face, realizing my life as I knew it was over. How could I have decided then? Fortunately, because we had discussed it, I was certain of Dee's wishes and said, "No." It was one of the hardest words I've ever uttered, but I've rarely regretted it. And when I do, cold logic tells me I would have been selfish to decide otherwise, for it certainly would not have been acting in Dee's best interests or according to her desires. Fortunately, there were no legal complications because my family stood with me—and because Dee had a living will.

The second time frame deals with your later life, starting moments after the death. If death occurs at home, you might have a little more time, but if it's in a hospital the nurses will pressure you to tell them your wishes on the "disposal of the body." This is no time to determine whether you want cremation or burial, and which funeral director you wish to be in charge. You are in a weakened state, subject to the tear-jerking spiels of scrupulous as well as unscrupulous operators. But if you've made these decisions already, you are not likely to feel second thoughts later. If the choice is cremation, you have to know what to do with the ashes. I have a friend whose wife died. She had specified with typical clarity a meaningful beach on which she wanted her ashes strewn. He knew he was following her wishes while spreading them, and derived comfort from the task.

What kind of a service does your mate want? Most will prefer a traditional one officiated by a member of the clergy, but others may desire a memorial based on general spirituality rather than attuned to some specific doctrine. Here I tend to deviate some from my admonition to respect the wishes of your partner. I still think these wishes are important and should be followed as much as possible, but the service also is for you and your family and friends. After all, you're the ones who have to go on, and you need this important ritual of closure to be healing for you. So, as you and your lover consider the service, strive as you've done so often before to find as many mutually satisfactory compromises as possible. What music would you/she both like? Do you/she both want friends and family to participate, either by readings or reminiscences? Do you/she both want flowers or do you/she prefer donations to a charity dear to you? Do you/she both want food provided after the ceremony? These and other questions can be resolved in a loving way, and later you'll be glad the decisions are made.

The planning of a funeral or memorial service is addressed in the comprehensive tome *Caring for the Dead: Your Final Act of Love* by Lisa Carlson. In addition to a wealth of general information, there is a description of the pertinent laws for each state. This book is especially valuable if you want something beyond the norm. Such individuality often runs afoul of funereal and bureaucratic intransigence, and this text indicates how you sometimes can circumvent the hurdles. My sister at one time was a Buddhist and had a strong desire for a traditional Buddhist handling of her body. There was initial concern that state laws would prohibit it, but she was able to find a funeral director who would accede to her wishes (and a lawyer to make sure he did).

How does your lover feel about donation of body parts? This is a horrendous decision if it has to be made on the spur of the moment. You must know ahead of time what to say when asked.

There are several additional questions that will arise eventually. They tend to be of less significance than those already discussed, but will be important enough that the surviving lover will desire guidance. While there are many possibilities, it's likely they will include the following: Who should receive specific objects? What about the eventual distribution of joint savings and investments? Is there any family history that should be recorded?

Perhaps one of the most important subjects to be discussed is that of a new mate. At first blush, this might appear to be a difficult area, but I suspect it's easier to consider when the current relationship is deeply loving. If you truly love your partner, you appreciate the wonder of that love and you want your lover to know it again. It will not be easy for him to form a bond with someone new. There will be feelings of embarrassment, worry, and guilt. If he has your blessing, it greatly reduces the effect of these negative emotions. My wife said to me well before she became ill, "It would be a real tribute to me and to our marriage for you to love again. It would mean our marriage was good for you." What a wise woman she was.

Now, once you've tackled these tough decisions together, it's time to have fun. Live your life with a gusto never before imagined, love each other with a lustiness surpassing even the vigor of youth, and treasure every moment you have together.

Key Points from Facing the Reality—the Later Years

- **Accept the inevitability of death.**
- **Create wills, living wills, and power of attorney documents. Name healthcare surrogates.**
- **Consider nursing home insurance.**
- **Discuss desire for resuscitation.**
- **Decide on burial or cremation (and disposal of ashes).**
- **Select a funeral director or a cremation service.**
- **Discuss the type of service and its details.**
- **Discuss donation of body parts.**

- Discuss disposal of property.
- Talk about the survivor accepting a new mate.
- Live every day to the fullest, as if it were your last.

Chapter 3

DIAGNOSIS—AND DEATH

She howled, "What shall I be without you?"

Possession by A.S. Byatt

For us, 1998 was not a good year. Dee's 97-year-old father, who had been diagnosed with lung cancer and subjected to debilitating radiation treatments, moved to an assisted-living facility. An independent, resourceful, and positive man, he immediately turned his room into a mini office, charmed the staff, and continued living his life as best he could. Using an archaic word processor, he produced several monographs on the history of education in Orange County, Florida, monographs that the local historical museum still sells. He exercised daily on a stationary bicycle and made so many phone calls they put in a special line just for him. Despite all the healthy activity, Dee saw this special man in her life slowly deteriorate.

Meanwhile, Dee's younger sister, Adelaide, was entering her own hell. Several years earlier, she had forsaken a hated law practice for a spiritually rewarding but financially devastating second career in counseling. When her economic situation became untenable, Dee offered office space and part-time employment at her behavioral medicine center. Soon after, Adelaide's health declined, mounting stairs became difficult, and early one morning her son called to report she was partially paralyzed and had been admitted to the hospital. She was diagnosed with lung cancer with metastases throughout her body. She initiated a regimen of imagery, journaling, and standard medical treatment in a Herculean effort to beat the odds. While recuperating at a nursing home, she, too, attacked life positively. She undertook to train the staff in kinder ways of dealing with patients. The result was more loving treatment of those with

Alzheimer's. To the surprise of all but Adelaide, not only the patient benefited, but so, too, did the staff because of significant reductions in the repetitive demands by the patients. Upon discharge from the nursing home, Adelaide moved to one of the rooms in Dee's center that we had converted to a bedroom. Adoring clients took their therapy by her bedside.

On June 30, 1998, Dee's father passed away. Adelaide, from a gurney, delivered a moving eulogy in front of several hundred. Twenty days later, Adelaide lost her fight. In the short space of six months, Dee had watched her father and her only sibling become ill from lung cancer, and, over a period of less than three weeks, die. Cancer had not had an impact on our family in the past, but now Dee became more attuned to its threat. I, naively, still clung to the belief we were a "golden couple," immune to all attacks on our health.

Despite my smugness, we, in March of 1999, sought legal and financial advice that resulted in revocable trusts, nursing home insurance, living wills, durable powers of attorney, and health care surrogates. We were so proud of ourselves, thinking we had all the "ugly" work completed and we could get on with the rest of our life together.

In December of the previous year, we'd both had a cough that lingered for weeks. Dee's never completely left, and in April 1999 blood appeared in her sputum. She feared it was cancer. Tuberculosis and other tests returned negative. A CAT scan interpreted by a thoracic surgeon evoked, with his typical sensitivity, "It looks like good old-fashioned lung cancer to me." The date was April 22, Adelaide's birthday.

With worst fears confirmed, we left the doctor's office in shock and terror. Long masters of our own fate, we now faced an extended period when others would assume control. Many of these medical practitioners were kind, understanding, and helpful. Others were insensitive, egotistical, and tyrannical. It probably would be difficult to find a team comprised of only the first type. Of course, you have every right to eliminate as many of the second as you can, but a couple of impediments block the way. This group may contain the most competent technically (our surgeon, for example), and the shock of the diagnosis and the need to get moving on treatment preclude extensive rational searches. So you're probably going to turn your medical treatment over to whatever group is available. If you're like we were, you're scared, frustrated, and angry, not knowing what's coming next. But you still have some power, the power of togetherness. We vowed to enter this fight as a couple, sharing the agony and, surprisingly, the joy—being with each other every step of the way. Don't underestimate the importance of this. It's a tremendous comfort to both.

If you're at this point and have not yet had the discussions mentioned in the previous chapters, now is the time. Procrastination is your enemy. In fact, now is the time to speak openly about the entire situation, including both your fears and your commitment to face jointly whatever comes. Don't be afraid to cry together, or vent your anger. Never has evasion-free honest communication with your lover been more important.

If you are the lover who is ill, there is much you can do to ease the situation for your dear ones, unfair as this may seem. For example, you can tell them you love them, that you are lucky to have played a role in their lives, and, if it's true, that you are prepared to die. A dear friend, knowing death was only weeks away, took concrete steps to ease the experience for her family. Each of her three young daughters received precious private time and, after her death, an individualized letter. Discussions with her devoted husband included tips on raising girls. Family conferences resulted in the distribution of special items— her engagement ring to one child, a diamond bracelet to another, her wedding ring to her husband. She made it clear she wanted husband and children to embrace whatever life offered, remembering her certainly, but also seeking new relationships and adventures. Perhaps surprisingly, none of this was morbid or difficult for her loved ones to handle. She couldn't have orchestrated a better result. This close family, obviously saddened by her death, nevertheless has been able to face its new world with a gusto that would meet with my friend's complete approval.

Paradoxically, it's important during this time of imminent death that you both continue to live: interact socially with others, go to movies, make love. Extract maximum benefit from every second. One friend joined other cancer patients in a local group called the "The Live Poet's Society" and wrote meaningful and moving verse. You may very well find that your love reaches heights during this period that could never have been imagined previously.

Over the next few months, I made bad choices, some of which bother me yet. I'll get to them soon. Hopefully my experiences will be instructive and perhaps save you some residual heartache.

Everyone is going to face life's challenges in his or her own way. A semi-professional artist, Dee produced a series of watercolors overflowing with emotions of the moment. The first, *Diagnosis,* in vivid color in the original, is reproduced here in black and white. Notice the horror, the fear, the helplessness. She showed it to me when I arrived home from work. I was disturbed and overcome by the power of the feelings expressed, and perhaps for the first time saw the insecurity and fragility of my normally strong wife.

I'm pleased to say my reaction was not one of my mistakes. I told her how I was affected, but emphasized I was thrilled she had put her feelings onto paper. I was so very proud of her. When she announced she intended to attempt a painting every day, I responded with enthusiasm.

Dee considered this art series to be one of her most important tools in dealing with the trauma of her illness. It included "pictures" of her disease, paintings done during a Paris trip taken prior to her surgery, "gratitude" paintings when we thought the cancer had been expunged, and a final tribute to Adelaide and her father in a "together again" setting.

In addition to her art, Dee employed several of the techniques taught in her program, including visualization. This was a tricky situation for her because she had to face the fact that she, director of a program dealing with people suffering from major diseases, had contracted cancer herself. Could she still be an effective guide to others? This turned out to be an unnecessary worry. She had never preached cures, although they often occurred. What she did teach was that every moment given to you should be lived to the fullest, whether it be for decades or days. This was the path on which she embarked, following the examples of her father, her sister, and her own teachings. And her clients turned out to be as supportive as anyone.

While the particular activities selected to help cope will depend on the individual, I think it's important to do something. Your lover may decide to write, run, meditate, bike, or combine any of myriad activities. At this point, you can perform a significant service by supporting whatever choice is made. Remember, she needs all the help you can muster.

Your support is essential not only here, but in *every* aspect of the fight. I was present during almost all the medical tests. During the entire two-hour MRI, where only Dee's feet extended from the banging and claustrophobic tunnel, I was standing rubbing her soles and massaging her toes. During the Positron Emission Tomography (PET) test, I sat by her side after signing a form relinquishing the hospital of responsibility if, for example, the radiation caused one of my ears to atrophy. Sometimes it took a good deal of cajoling, but I convinced the hospital to let me be present at all tests, except for one when I was thwarted by a young technician who didn't dare violate some bureaucratic policy. Furthermore, I attended all consultations with the surgeon, a competent and, I suspect (although I'm not sure), kind man, but one who probably for reasons of self-preservation was gruff, officious, and unapproachable.

What is important here is that it's essential for you to be a part of the entire procedure. I can look back on that time and know my role was significant, not only to Dee but also to me. Suppose, instead, I had left her to handle things alone because "I had to go to work" or "I can't stand to be in a hospital." I think I would be suffering a lot of guilt now.

There had been concern about "spots" on Dee's spine and neck. The tests, however, showed no threat from them so surgery was possible. It was scheduled for May 26. We visited our son and his family in Paris during the preceding week. The surgery to remove a lobe from Dee's lung was successful, pathology reported no lymph node involvement, and the surgeon announced no radiation or chemotherapy would be necessary. I believed him.

This was my first big mistake. I can offer the excuse that I'm not a medical person and would have no reason to doubt the doctor, the professional. Besides, we were so relieved to hear his opinion that we didn't give it a thought. But these are not excuses that will stand. In this day of the internet, anyone can obtain a mountain of material on any subject. Many doctors discourage this, essentially saying that a little knowledge is a dangerous thing. My response is that no knowledge is worse. I should have pressed for solid reasons why follow-up treatment was unnecessary, and for more information on the "spots." But neither Dee nor I did, and we blithely returned to our normal activities, albeit with a new sense of the fragility of life and the preciousness of our love.

Dee soon returned to work, painted a labyrinth on the concrete that constitutes our back yard, and created the "gratitude" paintings.

Sometime in July, the pain in her back increased. We all attributed it to the surgery. Indeed, the surgeon did nothing but prescribe additional pain medication and snappishly recommend we see our family doctor. Unfortunately, that wonderful, caring, honest, and competent man was immersed in a crisis of his own that resulted three months later in his leaving medicine. Consequently, he was rarely available and we were left with backups of questionable ability and commitment who did nothing.

And this is my second significant mistake. Why didn't I insist on another round of tests? Again, I can offer reasons, none of which help now. And I'm not sure Dee would have agreed to the tests anyway. But would they have been able to save Dee if we had acted? Our doctor said it was hard to say. We'll never know, of course, but I'll always wonder. If I had it to do again, I would insist that any new or increased pain receive immediate and detailed investigation.

The last week in July, I attended a professional conference and Dee, along with Rosalind, drove to North Carolina's shore to visit a friend. I've kicked myself repeatedly for leaving then, but the week was so spiritually healing for Dee that I think it was important for her to have that time.

The back pain increased during the first three weeks of August, and Dee began to lose control of one hand and a leg. If you get to this point, your mate will need extra love and, more practically, extra assistance. Don't shy from it, even if some of the tasks are unpleasant, perhaps assisting with bathroom functions. When faced with this duty, which bothered Dee greatly, I emphasized how lucky I felt that she could call upon me. And I told her yet again how much I loved her.

On Friday, August 20, Dee entered the hospital and began another round of tests. The MRI technician kept chastising Dee for moving. I finally snapped, "She's in pain. She's doing the best she can. Give her some credit!" I probably was more graphic, but at least the technician became a little less abrasive. Saturday evening, a neurologist, who had reviewed the scans, entered the hospital room and gently told us my beloved had devastating tumors on her back and on her neck near the brain. Remember the "nonthreatening" spots? We received the impression she had a few months.

When I left that night, I walked into downtown Orlando, immersed in a throng of 20-something revelers, unaware of my surroundings and not giving a damn if anyone saw the tears. The next day, Sunday, we discussed turning the dining room into a bedroom from which she could view trees and a lake, and also avoid the stairs to our normal chamber. That evening we considered, in consultation with our doctor, the health care team we would have. Because of her professional experience with the medical community, Dee had strong views about the oncologist she wanted and about those she wouldn't let anywhere near her. I spoke with our son, Geoffrey, who was by then in Miami. He asked if he should come. This represents my third and arguably worst mistake. I said we had some time, why not wait until we'd discussed the situation with the medical team, and I'd get back to him when we had more knowledge.

At 4 a.m. Monday, the hospital called saying Dee was "having problems" and wanted me there. I phoned Rosalind, who contacted her brother. I told Dee he was on the way and she said, "I hope he gets here." Then she continued, "I'm scared." I told her I knew. She died in my arms at 7:30, her daughter and son-in-law by her side. Geoffrey arrived at 10:00. The lesson? I should have played it safe and told Geoff to come on Sunday. What would have been the harm if he had, and then we still had the several months we thought would be ours? More than anything else, this deprivation of Dee's and Geoff's final opportunity to be together continues to haunt me. Not surprisingly, then, I strongly recommend visits not be postponed. The worst (best) that can happen is a great deal of time remains and further opportunities for contact are possible.

Dee was a remarkable woman, so her family "knew" she could beat this cancer. Just the day before, we all had agreed it was too early to give up. That morning, though, the situation was obvious. First my daughter, and then I, looked into her eyes and verbally gave her permission to go if that was what she wanted. It's a moment that will stay with me forever, and I think it helped bring her peace at the end.

Key Points from Diagnosis—and Death

- If you have not dealt with issues outlined in the previous chapters, do so now. Get your mate's (and your own) will, living will, health care surrogate, and power of attorney in order. Discuss funeral arrangements, disbursement of property, and any other details of importance to you both.

- Pick doctors you want. Don't let them intimidate you.

- Vow you will be with your lover through the entire process, and don't let the medical establishment thwart you.

- Talk, talk, talk. Be completely honest. Cry, vent, love.

- Support however your mate wants to attack the disease. State your opinions, but vow to accept her decisions.

- Live life as normally as you can for as long as you can. Do not let the disease make either of you a victim.

- Learn as much as you can about the disease, any associated surgery, and problems in recovery. If your doctor is secure, he will be helpful. Otherwise there's the internet, libraries, "ask-a nurse" hotlines, and myriad other sources. Check out your medical team.

- If a doctor tells you all is well, and you know there were problems of concern earlier, press to learn why they are no longer considered dangerous.

- If a new pain occurs or an old one flares, insist it be investigated thoroughly at once.

- Don't accept without question a doctor's prognosis, or allow him/her to discount your concerns.

- If death is indeed pending, and you are the one who is ill, try in any way you can to help your loved ones accept it.

- Don't delay getting people there who should be there.

- When it is time, and with all the love you can muster, give your lover permission to go whenever she is ready.

- Throughout the entire process, touch her often, hold her close, and never stop telling her you love her.

PART 2

PASSING THROUGH HELL TO RECOVERY

Chapter 4

The First 100 Hours

He had learned the worst lesson that life can teach—
that it makes no sense. And when that happens,
the happiness is never spontaneous again.

American Pastoral by Phillip Roth

Dee's breathing became inaudible as I cuddled her against my chest. I glanced at Rosalind, who nodded, her eyes sadder than I'd ever seen. I kissed my wife, my friend, my lover one last time. Having heard horror stories of dishonest missionaries of death, I gently extracted her rings, including her wedding band. It sounds so cold and calculating, but I'm glad I have them and I still keep them nearby. I told my daughter and her husband to take a last look, because they would never gaze upon her again.

A staff doctor entered the room after we left, apparently to poke and prod, to give official belief to the unbelievable. She emerged a few minutes later, saying, "There are no signs of life." I wanted to scream at her, "Say she's *dead,* damn you!" I don't know why I was so angry. Sure, I've always opposed cloaking hard issues in soft words. But I think the real reason is I didn't want the enormity of this personal tragedy mitigated by unfeeling strangers. Even then, though, I understood hospital personnel, including many doctors, are no more adept at dealing with loss than most of us. They all have their own issues about death. But I didn't care about anyone else's problems then. This was total devastation, and it was happening to me.

The nurses were professionally sympathetic, but clearly they were more interested in the benefits of an available bed than the despair of a bereaved lover. They said they needed to know about the "disposal of the body." Since I had not been wise enough to follow my earlier advice, I didn't know what to say. I knew Dee preferred cremation, but I had no idea which facility should handle it. I was angry already and didn't need what I considered to be undue pressure. I told the hospital staff they'd just have to wait and I'd get back with them as soon as I could. I couldn't leave yet. I re-entered the room alone, said a final goodbye to my beloved, and went home with my daughter and her husband.

If you're like me, there will be no easy time for you for quite a while. However, the first few days, until the funeral or memorial service is over, are so filled with necessary tasks and concerned friends and family that in some sense they are probably less unbearable than what follows. And food will not be a problem. It seems bringing nourishment to the bereaved is also nourishment for the giver. You and your family will eat well. It just won't taste as good as it should.

The first task was to select a firm to handle the cremation. How do you even begin? What difference does it make? Well, one difference is cost. My wife was a frugal woman whose penchant for saving allowed us to live at a higher level than our income warranted. She would hate spending more money than was necessary, and that was all the clue I needed. We phoned most of the places in the yellow pages and selected one of the least expensive. As far as I am concerned, the job they did was as professional as it could have been, and there was no hassle.

I was lucky to find a reputable crematorium, because this is a terrible time to be making decisions. And funeral homes know it. When selecting a casket for my mother a few years earlier, the salesman said one of the cheaper ones could not guarantee protection from the elements, implying, but not stating explicitly, that more expensive boxes would be better suited to the job. He said, "Do you understand what I'm saying?" I replied, "Yes. You're telling me bugs and animals are going to enter and eat her." I'm pleased to say he was somewhat shaken by the directness and later admitted even the more expensive units could not give the coveted guarantee. It is for reasons such as this, when you are so susceptible to manipulation, that it's best to have made these decisions ahead of the need.

Other seemingly unfeeling incursions may occur. The neurologist's office called saying they needed information for reimbursement. I meekly supplied it. Then they called again, asking for more. Again I complied. Then I got mad and hoped they would phone yet a third time. Would I give them a piece of my mind! They didn't, though. I suspect they didn't know of Dee's death. They weren't bad people. They had just contacted me at the wrong time.

There seemed to be so many tasks. What about the obituary? The crematorium delivered basic information to the local paper, but publication of additional details had to be purchased. Every day an obituary is printed about someone of special interest to the community, and a reporter friend thought Dee would be an appropriate candidate. Did we have a recent photograph? Yes, but it was in my office, necessitating a dash to the university, a clandestine entrance (I didn't want to talk to anyone there yet), and a rapid return.

What about notification of family and friends? Address book and Christmas list were produced. A few calls triggered an expanding network of the informed. At this point, the assistance available to you is an invaluable asset. There's an associated debit because this is when you hear the first of the comments that seem inappropriate. I'll mention a few later.

People Do the Best They Can

When people say incredibly stupid things, remember they wouldn't say anything if they didn't care. They lack one or more of experience, training, empathy or sensitivity. It's too bad. But our choice is to reject their overtures or to say, "Here is another person who is concerned about me." What they say doesn't help, but the fact that they want to say something does.

It's important to treasure these expressions of sympathy, no matter how inexpertly delivered they are. It means they care. It also is important to let others assist in any way you wish. They want to. It will help them deal with the lesser loss they are experiencing, and telling them what you need gives you a small feeling that you're still somewhat controlling your life. For example, assigning someone to buy several copies of the paper containing the obituary is a good move (I bought 10 and wound up keeping two).

What about the funeral? If you and your lover have discussed this, you know what to do and it's just a matter of details. Dee and I, of course, had not. But I did have a feel for what she liked. We planned an outdoor observance on the grounds of the center she had founded. I began with a few words, which I've reproduced in the Appendix. I almost completed them without breaking down, but lost it in the last few sentences. Then others spoke. More wanted to than the available time would permit. The final "speaker" was a world-class banjo player who led us in a couple of appropriate songs. We concluded with two chants, whose source is unknown to me, that Dee loved and had used in her work. They never fail to bring tears to my eyes:

From thee I receive,
To thee I give,
Together we share,
And by this we live.

and

Go in beauty,
Peace be with you,
We will meet again
In the light.

The chants were performed with the entire assemblage arranged in a giant circle, neighbor embracing neighbor. I went from person to person, giving each a hug and receiving one in return.

I realize that a memorial of the type that was right for us may not be what others want. But the goal is the same, to honor your lover and to help family, friends, and especially you to deal with the loss. And many of the possible mistakes that can occur are independent of the type of service.

Here's one mistake I made. Most people thought Dee's remembrance was a beautiful experience. An Indian friend said, "This is the way it should be." I think my son, however, would have preferred it to be a bit more traditional. Had I known then how he felt, I would have tried to satisfy his need. Had I known then what I understand now, I would have asked him explicitly about his desires. I've learned it's important to bring all close individuals into the planning process.

There are areas that seem less important, but attention to detail will avoid later disappointment. Of course, detail is hardly what you'll feel like dealing with at this time. Probably the best solution is to appoint someone you trust to handle them. For example, I wanted a guest book so I could know who had come. For church or funeral home services, this is not a problem. The professionals know how to deal with it, guiding arrivals to the signing table. We set up a book without assigning anyone to direct and didn't even think about the fact that there were multiple paths of arrival. Thus fewer than half the people signed. I spent the evening jotting down everyone I could remember who attended, but feel I missed some. Other factors may be important to you. This is another area where preplanning is beneficial.

Then there is the big mistake. Sometime on the afternoon of Dee's death, I received a call from the eye bank expressing sympathy and reminding me I'd been approached at the hospital about donating Dee's eyes. Actually, I hadn't been, and, when the caller realized that, he apologized profusely. I said I didn't want to donate, he was gracious, and we disconnected. The thought of violating her body was more than I could bear. It was the wrong time for that decision. Now I wish I had allowed it. I've been tormented ever since, second only to the sorrow I feel in delaying Geoffrey's arrival. I feel sure now that Dee would have loved this last caring gift by her. And I would have known a part of her still lived. Prior discussion would have made the decision significantly easier.

You'll get through these first few days, probably in a daze. You'll say the right things, do what is required, and be numb inside. And there will be times when the activity stops and the thoughts multiply. You'll be alone in bed. You'll cry, feel despair, perhaps want to die. I certainly did. I run more or less regularly, have for years. I distinctly remember arising early the morning after Dee's death, jogging to an isolated spot, and howling at the top of my lungs. I don't think anyone heard me, but I didn't care if they did. What did anything matter?

In spite of all the misery, it's important to be open to help. You may be an independent cuss who thinks accepting help is wimpish, unmanly, weak. If so, I hope you'll get over it. We all need help at *all* times, but especially at *this* time. A neighbor phoned the afternoon Dee died to say, "I know you walked with Dee every morning. I need some exercise and wondered if you'd like to go out with me." What a kind offer! As I'll indicate in the next chapter, I often just wanted to hole up and ignore the world. My first reaction was to refuse this generous gesture, but I did accept. We began the day after the memorial service and the association has developed into a treasured friendship with both him and his wife.

Once the service is over, friends and family members return to their lives, and you're left by yourself with your home, your memories, and your loneliness. This is when it really gets hard.

Key Points from The First 100 Hours

- **Don't be intimidated by hospital staff or other medical personnel. If you need extra time to be with your loved one and/or to think problems through, and it doesn't fit their schedule, ask them to wait.**

- **Remove all jewelry when you last see your lover.**

- **In the planning of the service, honor the desires of your lover, but also seek input from those most affected by the death.**

- **As much as is bearable, think about details so you will have the best possible memories of the service. If they have been a part of previous discussions with your lover, so much the better.**

- Treasure expressions of sympathy, no matter how misguided they may be in their presentation.
- Accept help from those who offer it. And feel free to request assistance.
- Know what you will do if the request comes for body parts.
- Feel free to cry, howl, and be angry.
- Recognize that despair and depression are normal reactions.

Chapter 5

THE FIRST 100 DAYS

And You Are ...?

One form offers the choices "married" and "single." Your hand dutifully causes the pen to check "single." Another permits "married," "single," "widow," "widower," and "divorced." That same hand records a check by "widower." "Single"! "Widower"! That's how the world knows you. But you don't recognize that person. Because your mind checked "married"!

You're on your own. The house is empty. And I mean really empty. You start to tell her about something you saw, then realize she's not there. You say "our" and "we" instead of "my" and "I." You recognize what you've done with a painful start that underscores your misery. And miserable you are.

The goal during this period is survival—whatever it takes. I could never presume to tell anyone how. What I can do is describe what I did, what helped me, with the hope that some of the experiences will benefit others.

This is not a good time to make major decisions—except for one. I didn't care if I were to die. I wanted to be with my Dee, forever. I dwelled on my death, wishing/willing its arrival. I don't think I would have proactively taken my life, but I would have welcomed an "accident" or a heart attack. Indeed, I ran extra long distances hoping I'd collapse. There seemed to be nothing to live for, no reason for continuing. It wasn't true, of course. If nothing else, my death on top of Dee's would have been devastating to our (yes I still say "our"—often) children. I think my daughter was especially concerned, so I made what I believe to be a wise promise to her. I pledged I would attempt to live for five years. I *knew* my despair would still be with me at the end of that time, yet the period was sufficiently long that there would be no immediate compounding of tragedy

31

for my loved ones. I also realized there was an unlikely prospect that I might feel better by then, perhaps even wanting to live. I made the same promise to my soon-to-retire doctor who had expressed concern about my depression. He wanted a lengthier commitment, but I refused any extension and he said he'd take what he could get.

I believe such a pledge is important, especially if suicidal thoughts pervade your mind. Such thoughts are not surprising, and the pledge helps channel them to a dormant stage without negating their validity. Once made, you must honor your promise by more than passive acceptance. True adherence requires pursuing healthy eating, exercise, and social habits—and *not* extra-long runs. Often you may not feel like making the effort, so it takes some willpower. So much has to be forced at this stage.

As I write this, it's more than four years since I gave my promise. Surprisingly, my outlook has improved. I still anticipate with pleasure my reunification with Dee, but the urgent desire to die has abated. But this is four years! There still are those first months to endure.

Much of the remainder of this chapter deals with methods for living up to the pledge. Other portions are concerned with handling the natural despair that pervades every moment of your waking thought. Remember the key word—SURVIVAL!

Rationalizations Don't Count

People tell you you're lucky to have so many fond memories—and perhaps you are. People tell you that time will cure all—and perhaps it will. People tell you that you should move on with your life—and perhaps you will. People remind you she wouldn't want you to suffer—and you know it's true. People tell you it was her time to go—whatever that means. There are many words people use to try to convince you logically that things will get better and you should put it all behind you. They don't matter. The pain, anguish, desperation, and misery remain, and that's okay.

At this time, well-meaning friends will offer care and advice of varied appropriateness. Soon, however, you'll realize that most of their comments show they don't have a clue how you feel. How could they? They haven't suffered such a loss. Exposure to death is not the same, unless it's of a lover, or perhaps a child. Certainly my mourning of parents and in-laws in no way approached the intensity of Dee's loss, nor prepared me for it.

There are those, however, who *have* been through it. Their advice is worth a listen. There are three instances in those early days that were pivotal, interestingly all from women: one who had lost her husband, one a daughter, and one a son. None were close friends, and one I had never previously met. Yet each took the time to contact me and minister in her own supportive way. The first sent me a short card indicating there are no acceptable words, and the only advice she could give was "to stay very, very busy." The second took me in her arms and said, "It will get better. I began to notice a change after the one-year anniversary." I'll mention the gift from the third person in a later chapter. I knew nothing would help me, including the comments of these kind people, but I also knew of their great loss. Maybe there was something to their words. I found them strangely comforting, in spite of doubting their validity. You simply can't ignore experience of that magnitude, and I strongly urge seeking the comments of those who have "been there."

I think the advice to remain busy is excellent. I was lucky. It was the beginning of the fall semester and, after a week in which others took over my classes, I returned to teaching. The workload was extensive, and completing it was mind-diverting and tiring. Of course, Dee remained on my mind every second—except when I was in front of a class. For precious 50-minute intervals, I could escape the demons. Find something to do that takes you outside your thoughts, that puts others first, at least for a short time.

Another required task allows no escape from the pain, but gives you an important opportunity to declare to others, and more importantly to yourself, that you're still functioning at some level. Expressions of sympathy will have arrived in many forms: letters, gifts, food, religious tracts. All, except for the mercenary few attempting to prey on your grief, are from caring individuals who want to help, including those who are unaware their particular words or beliefs are anathema to you. Each deserves an appreciative response. I had approximately 200 notes to write, and it took me well over a month. Every one was a reminder of my loss, but each also was a reminder of a person for whom Dee was important. That was comforting, and there was a feeling of accomplishment as the job advanced.

Things Are Not Just Things

"You're going to stay in that huge house by yourself?" the friend asks incredulously. "You'll want to get rid of her dresses as soon as possible," the well-intentioned acquaintance asserts. "Hide most of her pictures." "Do this." "Do that." Most people have advice on relieving the grieving, the implication being that the philosophy of "out of sight, out of mind" is wise and beneficial. Just the opposite is true. Love of many years does not change because of separation. One doesn't expect a serviceman's wife to rid her life of reminders of him when he goes to war for three years. Why is death any different? Her things are dear. Only you know when the time is right to get rid of them. And maybe that's never. Maybe you'll always keep a special dress hanging in the closet, her favorite book by the bed, or a portion of the scrumptious food she had left in the freezer. You have that right. If it feels right, it is.

As I've said, you'll find many who "know" the best way for *you* to get over *your* loss, and often their inspired suggestions would require significant changes in *your* life. The truth, of course, is your life has had quite enough change for a while. You don't need more. I decided to apply my earlier suggestion of making no major decisions, other than the one to stay alive, for a minimum of two years. I think this is important, again because this is a time of diminished rationality. There is a temptation to place trust in the "wisdom" of others since thinking for yourself seems so difficult. It's important to remember that rarely does a lifestyle change require immediate action, and by delaying you may avoid the heartbreak of a poor decision made in haste.

I believe routines are beneficial during trying times. I forced myself into a few, even though all I wanted was to lie around and cry. I continued to run three days a week. The daily walks with my neighbor lasted over a year. Exercise of some form is a wonderful way to make time pass, even when you hate it as much as I do. Dee preached journaling, so I thought I'd try it. Every day for well past a year, I wrote almost a page a day in a series of notebooks. They resembled letters to Dee more than outpourings of feelings, and looking back upon them they were certainly repetitive: "I love you," "I can't live without you," "I miss you," and other like phrases. I walked the labyrinth Dee had created twice a day, once early in the morning and once before I slept. I had promised Dee I would think positively every day about a couple of people who needed special help, somewhat akin to prayer. I kept that promise, and still do.

It's Not Enough!

You do all the right things. You journal. You run. You walk. You traverse the treasured labyrinth. You meditate. You send healing intentions to those in need. You accept every invitation you can. You take good friends to dinner. You treasure times with your children. You work. You force yourself to get up every morning to do all these. There is pleasure in much of it. But the agony, loneliness, despair remain.

In addition to the routines, there are social opportunities to snatch. I never refused an invitation unless there was a timing conflict. When someone phoned asking me out, my immediate reaction was to decline. Nothing sounded enticing. I was tired, and summoning the requisite energy usually seemed impossible. But I had made that pesky commitment to live, so I would force myself to accept. I dreaded leaving my home, but once out I almost always was glad I went. I imposed only one restriction. If the invitation was for a movie or play, I insisted it have a non-depressing theme. A comedy was best, but any good story with a positive twist was acceptable. My friends understood and honored my request.

It's important to continue to see those you have known as a couple. I'm aware of many who have felt uncomfortable being with the old crowd, and others who have said they were dumped because previous friends preferred to be with couples only. I suppose in some cases these views are accurate, but I think it's not in your best interest to assume they are. Instead, try to determine their validity. After all, these people have been your friends for years. True friendship transcends hardship. I wanted to maintain the relationships. If there is initial hesitation by couples about including you in their activities, it might be due to an incorrect feeling on their part that it would be too painful for you. Only you can fix this. I made it explicitly clear to my paired friends that I enjoyed being with them, liked seeing them interact as a couple, and that it didn't bother me, all of which is true. I think couples are great. After all, I was part of one for a long time.

Can't They Feel Your Pain?

The passerby wishes you "Good morning." The cashier sends you on your way with "Have a nice day!" Colleagues discuss your work. Friends tell you about their lives. And all the time, the anguish churns within. Can't they feel your pain? Of course not, and why should they? Their world goes on, just as yours used to, and somehow you continue to exist in it. You get up each morning and get through each day. Why bother? Why make an effort others can't fathom? Because there are those you love more than words can say and who love you. Because there are others you care about in special ways and who care about you. They want you to live. So you continue to, for them. But you don't do it any more for yourself. And that's your second huge loss.

So how did all my lofty actions help? Sadly, I can't identify a single action that eased the pain. The exercise was the dreaded time it always was. The journaling produced no psychological insights or physical relief. The supposedly inspirational labyrinth inspired me not at all. Its center, a power source according to Dee, was instead a source only of mosquito bites. Those receiving my daily positive thoughts, the two Dee had requested and other friends in special need, seemed to find no respite from their problems. All that resulted, after all this effort, was the passage of time and I was still miserable. Upon reflection, and only after many years have passed, have I come to wonder if the passage of time wasn't in itself a remarkable outcome. If your mind and body are occupied, time passes. That's progress at this point.

So you do all the "right" things and the despair continues. At this time, you might begin to notice that the solicitous behavior of family and friends begins to ebb. This is natural. They are returning to lives that have not been jolted to a new path. It doesn't mean they care less, only that their normal lives continue. But yours no longer is normal. It will never be the same again. It's important to accept this withdrawal by others, and to understand it. I was able to recall all the many deaths of friends and relatives I had experienced, and how I had returned to my regular existence fairly quickly. It's how we move on. But it's so much more difficult when it's *your* lover who is gone.

If They Ask, Tell; If They Don't, Don't

When good friends don't ask how you are, don't offer it gratuitously. They probably are uncomfortable and afraid of the answer. Accept their friendship and enjoy what they do have to offer. If they ask, tell them honestly what you feel. We all need friends who can accept where we are. If your answer makes them uncomfortable, you can give a palliative response in the future. If they accept the validity of your feelings, you've found a treasure.

Those who seemed so willing to listen before appear edgy when now you discuss your loss. They have other pressures demanding their precious time, or perhaps they simply don't know what to say and are uncomfortable, or maybe they're tired of hearing about your situation. They're polite, but you can feel the distance. The problem is you want to talk about her, need to. There are some options available to all, and we'll discuss them in the next chapter. If you're very lucky, as I was, some family and friends will be willing to hear you, and to accept your honest feelings. My daughter, who felt the loss as intensely as any child could, was always ready. So were my walking neighbors. Never did I detect a hint of unease, boredom, or déjà vu when I confessed to a bad moment or poignant memory. People such as these are rich finds. It's important to understand even they have limits, though. Accordingly, I was careful not to overindulge my craving for support. On the other hand, when I was speaking of Dee, I did not hold feelings back. These wonderful people have seen my tears and my anger, and they played an essential part in my survival during those horrible first months.

If you react as I did, there will be moments that are unbearable. These should be handled in any way you feel is right. I would go to the center of my house and scream with all my might. I'm sure the walls weren't as effective a damper as I would have wished, but no one ever complained. A neighbor did hear me crying once, though, as I walked the labyrinth, and he was moved to bring me a shepherd's pie. It was a beautiful and thoughtful gift, making me wish I ate red meat.

I was angry a lot. I raged at God, deciding eventually either He was powerful but not caring, or She was caring but not powerful, or It didn't exist. My mathematical mind could accept no other possibility. Four years later, I read the acclaimed *When Bad Things Happen to Good People* by Rabbi Harold S. Kushner in which he argues effectively for a caring, non-powerful God. I think his book is helpful, but whether it would be viewed as a comfort early in the grieving process will depend on the individual. I didn't need a caring God back then. I needed a miracle.

There are additional positive steps I found helpful. I wanted so badly to believe Dee remained in some form of afterlife. There are, of course, many books asserting its existence. Several of them recommend prayer as a way to assist a recently deceased in making the transition. I figured there was nothing to lose, and I did as suggested.

I also began to scrutinize my world for signs from her. After all, if there is an afterlife, it seemed only reasonable she would do all in her power to let me know she was all right. Every butterfly became an incarnation. Every light flicker was caused by supernatural powers. A particularly friendly pelican assumed monumental status. I started a list of possible signs, and now it approaches 100. With one exception, which I'll discuss later, every entry has alternative natural explanations. But at this stage I wanted to believe. And what's the harm? If you find comfort in searching for signs, I highly recommend it.

A friend who reviewed my manuscript told me she had found solace speaking to her lost husband. How could I have not included this comforting act in my first draft? On my daily labyrinth traversals, I tell Dee about my days, ask for her help with problems, and express my undying love. It seems to help.

I had a close call during this early period of mourning. I was exhausted mentally and physically. I seemed to sleep long and without interruption, but I awoke tired and stayed tired until dropping off at night. It was an exhaustion like none I had ever experienced. Normally fairly active, I would drag myself across campus. At the end of the day, I would trudge to my car. One afternoon, while driving home along an expressway, I dropped off. Just for an instant, and fortunately I snapped to attention in time to avert disaster. I don't know how typical I am with regard to this feeling, but I offer it so if you experience it you'll know you're not alone, and also as a warning to be especially careful when operating equipment. Remember, if you've made the promise to survive for five years, you have to take steps to make sure you do.

Somehow you get through the first few months. Everyone expects you to be back to normal. You begin to wonder if there's something wrong with you, because you still feel miserable. In the next two chapters, we'll explore dealing with the long term.

Key Points from The First 100 Days

- **Vow to make no avoidable major decisions for at least two years.**

- Make a solemn promise to someone you love that you will do all in your power to live at least five more years—and then conduct your life in the spirit of the promise.
- Listen politely to those who "know" what is best for you, and then ignore without guilt any of their advice, including mine, that you find not in accordance with your needs.
- Do listen to and consider comments from individuals who have survived a devastating loss. Then accept those ideas that seem valid to you.
- Find a way to be very busy with some activity that fully occupies your mind, at least for short periods.
- Respond in writing to all expressions of sympathy.
- Exercise.
- Find routine daily activities.
- Accept invitations, placing restrictions if you wish on the content of movies, plays or other forms of entertainment; and let your couple friends know you still enjoy their company.
- Be understanding when others return to their normal lives or seem uneasy discussing your loss.
- Be on the lookout for those rare friends with whom you can continue to be completely honest.
- Accept that it's normal and perfectly okay that you still feel bad, are still angry, and still use "we" and "our."
- If it helps, find an isolated spot and cry or scream or moan or whatever seems right. Recognize that intense feelings are reasonable.
- Pray for her.
- Search for signs that she is near.
- Be sensitive to the fact you may be emotionally and physically drained and thus must be especially alert when driving or operating any type of equipment.
- Do whatever it takes to survive, keeping in mind your pledge to live. Someday you'll be glad you did.

Chapter 6

The First Year

> ### "Enough" is When You Say it Is
>
> How long should you mourn? Is two weeks too much? How about four months? Isn't a year getting ridiculous? How long did you know her? A month? Two years? Forty years? Why should it take a shorter time to get over a love than it took to build it? Whatever time is required is right, and you and you alone can determine when or if the time has come.

The line I've drawn between the first 100 days and the rest of the first year is blurred and arbitrary. All suggestions of the previous chapter continue to apply. Major decisions still should be delayed, social contacts pursued, and established routines continued. At some point, though, you might notice a slight difference, the beginning of an acceptance, not of *what* happened, but more of the fact that it *did* happen. There are times you acknowledge she is not going to return, that you truly are alone. It doesn't make you feel better, but it is a step to recovery.

It may not seem like it, though. After all, you're still miserable and wonder if you'll ever feel otherwise. If you're like me, you might not even want to emerge from those hideous depths. To do so seemed an unfaithful act to me. Wasn't I demonstrating my love for my mate by never progressing beyond the mourning? I knew Dee would have been disgusted by such an attitude. Logic also argued against my feelings. In disagreements between emotion and logic, however, feelings almost always triumph, and no one was going to keep me from being wretched the rest of my life.

The problem was that promise I'd made to my daughter about living five years, and my commitment to acting in the spirit of it. Because of Dee's work,

I knew several caring therapists. One of them, who worked at her center, suggested we get together for a talk. He emphasized it was not a therapy session, that he needed it as much as I because he, too, felt a loss. I'm glad I took him up on his offer. I told him how I felt and he said I was depressed, and that it wasn't surprising. He said there's a rule of thumb that it takes anywhere from one to two months *for each year of being together* to fully return to normal life. At least this was validation of the way I was feeling. In my case of 42 years of marriage, this translated to between 3½ and seven years. It seemed a bit short to me, but notice how well it tallied with my five-year promise. There is, of course, nothing concrete about any time period. We are all different. But it is verification that lengthy mourning is normal, despite what well-intentioned friends may feel and some books state.

Although I didn't pursue counseling myself, I think it's worth giving the idea serious thought. This becomes especially true if you don't have the special friend with whom you can confide, and then confide again, and yet again. Or if your dark thoughts wind up controlling every aspect of your life. The right therapist can help ease your mind about the extended duration of your grief. Recognize, though, that if a therapist becomes directive or unfeeling, he or she is not the right one for you. Some counselors are caring and sensitive. Others are not. Most of them will not have experienced the type of loss you have. If you get one you don't like, look elsewhere.

I know there remains a stigma about accepting the need for counseling, especially with men. All I can say is, "Get over it!" It's silly, even stupid, to turn your back on a source of possible comfort. And there is nothing macho about embracing stoic misery in place of rehabilitating assistance. Remember, if you don't like the counseling, you can always quit. There's nothing wrong with that either—as long as you entered into it with an open mind.

In the same vein, you might try a support group. Several exist explicitly for those experiencing loss. They allow honest expression of feelings in a safe setting with others in the same boat. Funeral homes often sponsor them and, even if they don't, are a good source of referrals. Occasionally one-time events are planned. I went to two. The first, held at an outdoor amphitheater, mimicked a revival meeting with "testimonials" from those who have survived. The second, held at a church shortly before the Christmas following Dee's death, was facilitated by an expert from outside the area. Neither event was particularly helpful to me, but I was amazed at how well some of the participants were adjusting. On the other hand, many looked as miserable as I felt. But I started wondering if maybe I should be doing better. The facilitator at the church knew something about this, though, because he gave us each a certificate reading:

Permission to Mourn:

The holder of this certificate _____ is hereby entitled to publicly acknowledge their loss, mourn openly, to share narratives of the loss, and to recruit social support in their own way and time, without apology or embarrassment. Tears, memories, silence, uncertainty, and strong emotions are hereby enfranchised. Please treat this griever with kindness, compassion, and love. **This certificate has no expiration date.**

The bold of the last sentence is mine. What could be a greater validation of the normalcy of long-term mourning than this certificate? I inserted my name and posted it in my office, where it remained until I retired, almost four years after Dee died.

Most libraries house a host of books on loss and grieving. I read voraciously, but for the most part found little comfort in them. One notable exception is *On Life After Death* by Elizabeth Kübler-Ross. It gave me great, if short-lived, moments of peace to realize a scientist of her caliber is convinced death is simply a step into another life. What a concept! Of course, it violated every gut instinct this technically trained guy had. A mathematician's job is to accept nothing unless it can be proved rigorously. Life after death falls woefully short on verifiability. My fascination with Kübler-Ross's book is a measure of how desperately I wanted to cling to the possibility that Dee still existed on some plane. It was the same desperation that made me interpret two swans appearing without reason on a local lake as manifestations of Dee and her sister, Adelaide. Little did I know just how far I was willing to pursue this concept of an afterlife.

A short time later, the third woman mentioned earlier who had sustained a terrible loss performed a courageous and deeply appreciated act. Just a couple of months before Dee's death, her intelligent and talented son had passed away in his sleep from a cause no one was able to determine. Deep in her own grief, she heard about my situation and requested an opportunity to talk with me. She didn't know me, but we had a mutual friend, the mate of my neighboring walker. I couldn't imagine what she might want, but I agreed to a meeting.

She began by apologizing if she was intruding, but also saying she had heard about Dee and for some reason she didn't understand, felt compelled to see me. She continued by describing her visits to a medium in nearby Cassadaga, an internationally known spiritual community about 30 miles from Orlando. I didn't know what to think. With the superiority of a scientific know-it-all, I had all my life spoofed the concept of communication with the dead (those in "spirit," as they say), although in the back of my mind there was a small imp muttering, "Yes, but wouldn't it be nice if it were true?" What was clear to me was my visitor was an intelligent, caring, and brave woman who wanted to share an experience she had found comforting. I thanked her warmly for her concern and promised I'd give the idea serious thought.

I'm not sure how true that promise was at the time I made it, but the possibility became a persistent pest. I'm sure it was kept alive by the desperate need to stay in touch with my beloved. A few weeks later, I made an appointment, informing the medium my mind was open but I had serious doubts. She replied that an open mind was good enough for her.

I left for my "reading" wondering if I'd be visiting a turbaned, black-robed hag with crooked teeth, crystal ball, shaking tables, mysterious sounds, and darkened parlor. What I discovered was a soft-spoken, kind, and refined grandmotherly woman in her 60s, a chair for her, a sofa for me, and a comfortable well-lighted drawing room. I was with her for *three hours!* I thought, oh boy, she's going to sock it to me with her fee. But she charged exactly what she'd quoted me over the phone, which was less than what many mediums expect for half an hour. By no means was I blown away with what I heard. There was no one "communication" that said, "Yes, it really is Dee visiting." There were several small 'successes,' each of which could have been a good guess made by an astute observer of my reactions and vulnerability. If there was a telling experience, it was in the aggregate of these minor comments. What was the probability of guessing right on all? Of course, there were some statements that were way off, verifying my doubts. When I got home, I recorded all of the comments, right and wrong, that I could remember, and was amazed at the number that were correct. I returned to the same medium once more, but the second visit was less satisfying.

I have an acquaintance who is actively involved in "mediumship" and has contacts with "the best mediums" of England. She brings them over for tours, and I've seen two of them, each for half-hour sessions. They both, one a man and the other a woman, have been pleasant and caring. Each encouraged recording the session, and each came up with "communications" that were right on the money and others that were way off. But some of the right ones seemed truly amazing to me. As an example, what type of vegetation do you suppose my wife would have loved? Go on, take a guess before you read on. Most would have to select randomly, and a certain percentage might predict gardenias, which would have been correct. I'll speak more about gardenias later. So a message about that perfumed flower would have impressed me, but as usual I would have qualified my enthusiasm by considering it a lucky guess. But that isn't what one medium said. What she communicated is that Dee wanted me to "take care of the fig tree." I suspect very few would have conjectured the juicy fig. Yet Dee loved figs and we had a notoriously unproductive tree on our property. I was indeed blown away by this.

I wouldn't blame you if you scoffed, thinking I've gone over the edge. I don't recommend that this is something everyone should do, or claim there is any validity to it. It certainly goes against my very nature, and in my few visits I was acting uncharacteristically. I have never returned for additional readings. However, if you want to pursue such an adventure, I recommend the book *The Afterlife Experiments: Breakthrough Scientific Evidence of Life After Death* by Gary E. Schwartz with William L. Simon. Schwartz is an established scientist at the University of Arizona who embarked on a study of mediums, originally expecting to show they did not possess special powers. He conducted what sounds to me to be scientifically designed experiments that show a statistically significant ability on the part of talented mediums to accurately divine messages from a departed soul. They also show these mediums are not perfect.

Please do not interpret my comments as an endorsement of mediumship. I still have many doubts, but I have learned to keep an open mind, probably because I want so much for Dee to remain close. I offer it as an idea that would never have occurred to me without suggestion from elsewhere. And, you might ask, what's the harm, especially if you derive some comfort from it?

Actually, I think there *is* potential harm, but it can be avoided if you're careful. I certainly am no expert on the subject, but I am confident you must not overly rely on the medium or communication from "the other side." Take it for what it is, a possible source of comfort. It is *not* a guide to life. Go only to reputable mediums. All I've seen have been recommended by people I trust. If one discusses a curse on you, or says you must return regularly (for additional money, of course), or you have the slightest feeling of discomfort, run to the nearest exit and don't look back. The honest mediums I saw discouraged dependence, did not take advantage of me, honored doubts, and didn't play tricks. Be as skeptical as you want. Or ignore the entire idea.

Inevitably, anniversaries and holidays arrive. There are all the familiar ones with their memories. Now there's a new one, the anniversary of her death. I remember thinking one day (one week, one month) ago she was breathing. And then she wasn't. My birthday fell less than a month after her death, and it meant so little to me. Hers was 20 days later and I shed many tears. I was invited to my son's for Thanksgiving. His father-in-law, Herb, had died about a month before Dee. Both grieving families gathered for the festivities. All I wanted to do was speak about my loss, but no one said anything. It seemed to be total denial.

Finally, my daughter proposed a toast to Herb and Dee, an act that relieved the pressure on me to include Dee somehow in the festivities.

These special days are difficult. They still are for me. I always want them to have significant meaning, to be a reminder of what Dee and I had and how we had enjoyed celebrating them together. I don't want to forget the many happy memories, and I don't think I will. There is always some pain, but it is beginning to mitigate. In the beginning, though, it was very tough. Do whatever it takes to get through. On that first birthday of Dee's, my neighbors invited me and other good friends to breakfast and we sang happy birthday to her. I still remember the loss and pain I was feeling and the tears flowing down my face, but I considered this a beautiful tribute to her and I remain profoundly grateful for the thoughtfulness shown.

Keep as many traditions as you wish. There is no need to make changes, but do create new "traditions" when it seems right. Here's a small one of mine: At Christmas, we always had a large tree. The thought of continuing that, with all its special memories, has been too much for me. Since her death, I have employed a three-foot approximation and have been satisfied with it.

One other tradition I initiated that first Christmas was to have Dee give me a gift. That year it was an electric razor. It was wrapped in our finest paper and placed under the miniscule tree. Such gifts appear not only during the Yule season, but also on my birthday and Fathers' Day, each with a short note of love from her. So far they have included various tools and computer software, and for one birthday a digital camera. They always are items I would feel guilty about spending money for, which means they are exactly the type she would have been sure to get me. Strangely, I have found this seemingly bizarre practice to be extremely comforting, and every time I use one of these special gifts I think of Dee and my heart fills with love. I also have noted that the charges always appear on my credit card, so at least in this area things haven't changed that much.

It is worth re-emphasizing that, as you approach the one-year anniversary, it is normal and understandable to remain grief-stricken, angry, and despondent. Recall the "one to two months per year of being together" rule-of-thumb. Nevertheless, you probably will find the tears flowing less, the mind concentrating on other things, and the moments of enjoyment increasing. At some point, you begin to believe you have a future, and the fact that you do is in no way a sign of disrespect to your lover.

Key Points from The First Year

- Accept that continuing to feel bad is normal, that there is no timetable for "getting over it."

- Remember you have the right to grieve, for as long as necessary.

- Continue to delay major decisions, keep up with social contacts, and maintain routines.

- Consider counseling, support groups, and special events that deal with loss.

- Read books you find helpful; discard those you don't even if they were recommended by friends.

- If exploring the possibility of life after death appeals to you, read about the subject, look for "signs" from your loved one, and decide if seeing a reputable medium is right for you.

- Recognize it is normal for anniversaries and holidays to be difficult.

- Keep all the traditions you have loved that are still comfortable for you. Discard those which no longer seem right, and create new ones, all without the sense of any betrayal of your past.

- Think about giving yourself gifts from your loved one on special days.

- Don't feel guilty as you start to feel better. Realize this is what your lover would want.

Chapter 7

THE NEXT FEW YEARS

Life

Life! Her! You embraced it passionately—just as you did her. You inhaled its beauty, opportunity, adventure and enjoyed it fully—just as you did her. You searched for its every nuance—just as you did her. Life! Her!—Her! Life! Inseparable! You used to want to live forever—with her. You were an active participant in life—with her. Now you're only a spectator—without her.

Time in its inexorable way passes, and the difficult one-year anniversary of her death is endured. These annual remembrances remain difficult for me, but they are getting easier. In fact, after that first anniversary, I began to think a little about my future, and what the rest of my life would be like. I recalled the statement by one of my mentors that she found the heaviness begin to lift after the initial year. I also recalled how little faith I had that the same would apply to me. But it did. Time is an amazing healer.

I don't mean to imply that suddenly all is well, the past is forgotten, and the future beckons with enthusiasm. Far from it!

I never want to forget the past. I keep pictures of Dee where I can see them easily. Immediately after her death, I had photos everywhere. I wonder now what visitors thought. These days, a few are sufficient. Her ashes remain in a box in my bedroom, waiting to be joined with mine. More on that later. Every few years, I refurbish the labyrinth she created, and I continue to walk its path daily. It's my time to be with her, and when I reach the center, that location of powerful energy—according to Dee—I always am hopeful of some contact with her.

> ### Memories
>
> The first date. The first kiss. The fights. The making up. The marriage ceremony. Birth of the first child—a son. Two uncompleted pregnancies. Birth of the incredible daughter. Raising children. Years of loving and caring and learning. The horrible year. The rediscovery of love and its rebuilding to incredible levels. The years with just the two of you. The mutual support. The exultations in the other's achievements. The unfilled retirement plans. The illness. The recovery. The moment of death. Each memory brings tears—unbidden and uncontrollable. But you wouldn't give up one to ease the current pain.

Alas, it was a hope long unfulfilled. By the time of our wedding anniversary, almost two years after her death, I had given up. I walked the labyrinth, reached the center, paused as I always do, and attempted to create an empty mind—and was assailed by the unmistakable odor of gardenias, Dee's treasured flower. Within seconds, the smell disappeared. I couldn't believe it. I scoured the area attempting to find the source. Certainly not in our yard, where the plants mocked me with their barren stems, nor anywhere else I could discover for several blocks. I'm not wrong. I did smell gardenias. And the next day it happened again, just for a few seconds. The day after that, I attacked the labyrinth with unrestrained enthusiasm. Nothing! And there has been no repeat since, not even on the next five of our anniversaries. If someone had told me this story, I surely would have scoffed, and you can make of it what you will. I'm convinced it was a communication from Dee, and I remain hopeful there will be more in the future, even though it is now well over half a decade since the last.

I'm not the only one who has received signs. A no-nonsense "prove-it-to-me" type of guy whose wife died was visiting the New York Public Library. For some reason he couldn't fathom, he was drawn to a room housing an art exhibit and, furthermore, to a specific painting in that room. A glance at the title showed it to be virtually identical to the name of a location on the South Carolina shore that had special spiritual meaning to him and his wife. He is convinced she guided him to the art. An interesting book, *Hello from Heaven!* by Bill and Judy Guggenheim, details similar experiences. While this volume does not have the scientific foundation of the Schwartz work, it still may be of comfort to the grieving.

The pain of Dee's loss has not disappeared. Nor do I want it to. I want my memories to remain vivid. She was my life for 44 years. I refuse to relegate that experience to oblivion. However, now the memories bring laughter more than tears, comfort more than torment, peace more than turmoil.

"Why?" Is A Reasonable Question— But The System Stinks

Why did she have to die? Why would any reasonable, caring God allow this to happen; or allow children to be hit by a car; or allow earthquakes, tornadoes, hurricanes, floods to kill thousands of innocents; or allow a murderer to wipe out an elderly man on a whim? Why does some scumbag live to a ripe old age and she dies in the prime of life? Why would she be taken when there is still so much good left for her to do? All valid questions, and you have a right to the answers. But you won't get them. So you have to live without knowing. How? If you figure it out, tell me.

I think the message here is simply a continuation of what has been mentioned repeatedly. What is right for you is right. There is nothing wrong if you still grieve. I remain angry at times. I wonder why Dee had to be taken when she was unselfishly accomplishing so much good. I still am hurt by the fact that I never seem to dream of her. A couple of years ago, I was walking across campus when a sob erupted, seemingly from nowhere. Subconsciously, I had been thinking of Dee. Recently, a neighbor mentioned her and my tears flowed. I thought I was beyond that, but I'm glad I'm not. I am unembarrassed by these continued displays of affection and loss. Caring people will understand.

Coupled with the grief, though, was a definite shift in thought patterns. While before I continued life in a way that approximated as much as possible how it had been with Dee, I started to question both the physical layout of my surroundings and the manner in which I carried out my everyday activities. I made no radical changes, but I no longer accepted the old as best for my altered circumstances. I eventually reached the point where major decisions could be considered. The ban on them approached an end. The biggest decision I've made to date may not sound earth-shattering, but it has surprised many. I have a large home, and for several years I was its only occupant. My decision was to remain in it as long as possible. I love it. I love the neighborhood. And I love the memories. Others under similar circumstances have elected to move, perhaps to escape those memories. We're all different, so it's not surprising we make different decisions. What is important is that the decision is delayed until sufficiently long after the loss of your lover so you know it's based on what is best for you. Now is the time to start consideration of new paths.

Humor is a wonderful pain pill, and I think it's important to seize it whenever you can. Dee and I always did. Even in the darkest early days after her death, I couldn't bypass the opportunity to mock commercials, inflict awful puns on friends, and make fun of myself. As time went on, I was able to recall some of the outrageous statements made to me by well-meaning individuals and to laugh at the incongruity of it all.

And The Winner Is ...

The entries were many, and the judges of the tasteless comments contest had a difficult decision. The second runner-up is, "I know it was hard, but it's all behind you now." The first runner-up, and what at first looked like a sure champion, was uttered three weeks after her death: "Are you dating?" Only the following entry, the winner, could have surpassed it: "It must be nice having two cars now." It takes all you have to accept the statements for the caring behind them. Try to see the humor in them, for there's little enough of that these days.

Also, if you're attracted to the idea, assisting others is a terrific way to help ease your grief. I'm sure my three mentors mentioned earlier derived some comfort by presenting me with their wisdom. My job afforded me a ready-made opportunity, and I would spend hours listening to students about personal problems far from mathematics. While not feeling especially wise, I think the fact I was there in a non-judgmental role was beneficial. There are many organizations that are begging for volunteers. Such work not only brings satisfaction, but also opens the door to increased social contacts.

Two significant questions arose in this period of my grief: What would I do with all of Dee's things? And should I consider a new love? Both of these can result in considerable inner turmoil, and the next two chapters are devoted to them.

Key Points from The Next Few Years

- **Don't expect a curtain to rise, magically revealing a new and glorious life.**

- Don't feel anything is wrong with you because you still grieve and have moments of anger.
- Cherish the memories, and attempt to derive comfort from them. Allow them to help you heal.
- Remain open to signs from her: a special smell, a poignant dream, a previously agreed-upon message, or anything having significant meaning.
- Search for and enjoy the humor and absurdity in your life.
- Consider volunteer work.
- Start to think about the delayed major decisions.
- When you're ready, allow yourself to evaluate changes in lifestyle and/or surroundings, keeping in mind that what worked when you were a couple may not be best suited for you alone.
- Be alert to subtle differences in your attitude about life, and use them as prods to advance the recovery process.

Chapter 8

CLEANING HOUSE

Decisions

The dress will attend no more parties. The book is forever closed. The thyme, old and soggy, has doctored its last meal. Memories—one box for Goodwill, one for the library, and the other for the city dump.

Dee was a pack rat! Every cubic centimeter designed for storage stored. Drawers were jammed, closets overflowed, and more than 30 flea market reading glasses dotted tables, chests, floor, and crevices between sofa cushions. Food proudly displaying labels 10 years old lined the rear of refrigerator and freezer, dozens of containers of solidified spices stood at attention three deep on shelves, and books filled hundreds of linear feet of cases. There were more than 20 pairs of scissors, four score skeins of yarn, and 18 boxes crammed with patterns. Notebooks stuffed with journal articles and penciled comments surrounded every chair in which she sat. This seeming bedlam provided the nurturing environment from which Dee produced unique home decoration schemes, delicious and nutritious meals, beautiful clothes, detailed family holiday plans, innovative therapeutic modalities, and an internationally hailed book. What was chaos to me was fertilizer to her.

While not a neat freak, I operate in a different manner. My part of our world—desk, shop, attic, basement—tended to degenerate more slowly and rejuvenate more often. I don't like to spend 20 minutes hunting a pair of pliers. Fortunately, we each recognized the way the other lived was part of the "small stuff," and our different styles managed to coexist without conflict, at least most of the time.

I would give anything to have the reason for that clutter back. For two years after her death, I continued to embrace and endure it, for the most part leaving the chaos unchallenged. After all, didn't it prove I was faithful to her if I maintained the status quo? And if that were true, then wasn't it clear what it would mean if I made changes?

It took that two years for me to begin to realize I really was not maintaining the status quo. Everything had been forever altered by Dee's death. That status quo wasn't, and there wasn't a damned thing I could do about it. Except to continue living, forging a new lifestyle that meshed with the new circumstances. I finally came to understand that changes did not dishonor my lover. Indeed, she, who always was examining her own directions in life, would be thrilled to see me do the same. Why was that so hard to comprehend? Slowly I started to question former practices, deciding some withstood the test and should be continued while others could be abandoned. It was the start of my new life, a life still with Dee but also uniquely my own.

I've said I have a big house. What I really had was a big house chock full of objects I never would use. Emotionally I was tied to the past, but rationally I realized it was time to restructure. Partially I was motivated by recollections of the effort required to close houses owned by my mother, Dee's sister, and Dee's father after their deaths. I wanted to spare my children as much of that chore as possible. With my daughter's help, we started going through each room, separating items into "keep," "donate," "gift," and "toss." I had no trouble with the "keep" pile. But each entity in the other categories was more than unwanted trash—it was a memory of shared love.

I think I would have eliminated less than half of what we finally settled on if it had been left to me. My daughter, though, kept me on track. She'd ask if I had used an item in the last two years. Most often, I sheepishly was forced to admit it had remained untouched and unnoticed for 20 years. Then she'd ask if I foresaw a need in the future. Her irrefutable logic triumphed and the object went. You can imagine how long this process took if each item induced such individual trauma, especially since we rarely worked more than 15 minutes on any day. The work required over two years to complete. Now I'm starting a second pass—on my own this time.

Some clearing tasks, such as attacking the refrigerator, involved negligible emotional stress. For example, tossing a plastic bag containing unspecified decaying green substances posed no problem whatsoever. Other categories, though, gave pause.

Her jewelry was one. What should I do with all her pieces? A very few were valuable and they were easy. They went to my daughter. For the most part, Dee preferred a multitude of inexpensive baubles giving her daily variety. Drawers were filled with 25-cent shell and beaded necklaces discovered at yard sales, pins of all shapes and sizes, and enough rings to adorn a millipede. When I looked upon them, I didn't see cheap jewelry. Instead, my mind created visions of her excitement when she purchased these items, and how she looked with them on. I could not throw them away. But I found I could distribute them to those close to her. I discovered comfort in the fact that others would enjoy a special part of her.

This concept of permitting Dee's friends to select objects that were important to her allowed me to feel I was accomplishing more than simply ridding the house of her things. I also was extending her memory. I employed the same approach with Dee's clothes. For some reason, I did not have the same difficulty with her garments that I did with her jewelry, with one exception. Dee loved colorful scarves and wrap-around skirts. She either would pick them up wherever she found them or make them from the "perfect" piece of discovered material. She wore them to work virtually every day, as well as in the evening and at weekend events. To my mind, they were a part of her essence. My daughter and I collected all of them—there must have been 50 of each—and placed the scarves in one box and skirts in a second. Then I carried the boxes to every female I could think of who was important to Dee, and let her pick what she wanted. People were delighted! Despite due diligence with this task, I still have many left. They will remain in their respective boxes until I am successful in finding appropriate homes. As far as Dee's other clothes are concerned, I selected a couple of outfits that I particularly liked and keep them in the closet that was once hers. I have no intention of ever discarding them. The rest we sorted, placing most in boxes for a yard sale, but selecting some we thought special friends might enjoy.

Since clothes are such personal items, I think there is a tendency to feel guilty about weeding them out. Perhaps that's why I waited almost two years before taking tentative stabs. As always, though, the guilt is a negative your lover would beg you to abandon. Wait until the time is right for you to start the cleanup. It could be months or years. But when you do attack it, do so with the knowledge that your partner approves.

We had two cars. After four years, I sold one, keeping the Camry she loved. I'm glad it is her car that remains, but I kept it because it was the better of the two. Boxes and boxes of china which I will never use, can't develop any interest for in my children, and have too many memories to let go of remain in storage. Love letters dating to 1955 and unread for more than 50 years are boxed in my attic. Scrawled on the box is an admonition to my children to destroy without opening. I don't think I will ever be able to read them again, but I simply can't throw them out. The litany about clearing my home of the past could stretch for pages, but the gist of the possibilities has already been covered.

There still was the question of what to do with everything you've decided to eliminate but haven't given to special people. My solution has been three yard sales and donations to Goodwill; the local, university, and public school libraries; and the county historical society. The money earned from the sales was given to charity, a final gift from my wife.

Near the beginning of the task, I mentioned its undertaking to a friend. Perhaps sensing my ambivalence and wishing to ease my mind, he said, "This *was* your and Dee's house. But now it is *your* house." He is a kind man, and it was presented in a kind way. But it didn't ring true. Ignoring the joint ownership struck me as relegating the wonderful memories to the past, when I want to hold them in the present. My own feeling is that it *was* and *is* Dee's and my home jointly, and also it *is* my home alone. And nowadays it *is* my and someone else's home. All three ownerships can coexist simultaneously, in my mind, with combined love and satisfaction.

As a part of this entire "cleansing" process, I am leaving as much information as I can to my loved ones to assist them in settling all aspects of my estate as easily as possible. For example, I am making a list of categories of items in each room with what I hope are useful comments for when my children must deal with them: "toss without worry," "this may be valuable so try to sell it," and "this has too much meaning to me to discard, but there is nothing of value and it can be heaved." When there is a special story attached to an item, I include it. I also am placing financial and additional information on paper so they'll know about my bank accounts, my desire for cremation and the distribution of my ashes, what I would like in my memorial service, and other wishes. My goal is to make life as easy as possible for my loved ones during a difficult time that I now hope will be many years down the road.

The project described in this chapter began with trepidation and guilt. However, as it approached completion, I had a feeling of tremendous accomplishment, realizing I had maintained important memories of Dee while freeing myself from the stagnation caused by ill-advised attempts to live in the past.

Key Points from Cleaning House

- Be willing to consider transformations in your lifestyle.
- Recognize your lover would want you to change in ways that are comfortable for you, and would not want you to feel any guilt.

- Clear out objects as much or as little at any time as you wish. There is no hurry.

- Give items special to you and your lover to special friends.

- Keep as many of her clothes as you wish, for as long as you wish.

- Consider donating as much as you can to worthy organizations.

- Consider having garage sales and giving proceeds to a charity favored by your lover.

- As you make changes, keep those items and memories that you want and which are intimately tied to your lover, but feel free to create an environment which is uniquely yours.

- Leave specific information for your loved ones regarding your finances, wishes regarding burial or cremation, directions for your funeral or memorial service, and anything else of importance to you or which will ease their job when you are gone.

Chapter 9

LOVING AGAIN

New Love?

People ask if you're dating, and the idea seems abhorrent. Others tell you she would want you to. She may have said so herself, indicating it would be the greatest tribute to your marriage if you could love again. You see a friend remarried after little more than a year following his wife's death, and you wonder how, even as you rejoice in his happiness. So what's wrong with finding a new mate? Absolutely nothing! If that's what happens to you, proceed without concern and make the most of every second. On the other hand, if another love is of no interest at the moment, don't feel you're wasting your life, the precious time you have left. The original love is too strong and can't be put aside quickly—or at all. Like so much else in this grieving process, whatever seems right for you is right for you.

"Are you dating?" It's hard to believe, isn't it, that a friend posed this three weeks after Dee died? You could have flown a kite into my jaw-dropped mouth. She laughed and said, "You should see your face!" Words almost never fail me, but I was paralyzed. It was an extraordinarily insensitive remark, but it does speak to an important possibility that must be faced eventually. Just not at three weeks!

I, of course, was convinced I never wanted to be with another woman. Dee was my life partner, and she still was and always would be, even though she was gone. Period! Dee wouldn't have approved of such a declaration. She had been explicit during happier days that she wanted me to marry again if anything happened to her. As I've said before, she had indicated it would be a tribute to the relationship we had if I were to take on a new love. I believe, though, she would have considered three weeks a bit early.

Over the years, I had observed others in my situation dealing with the question of a new relationship. Some friends had remarried and created a second happy life. It always was a joy to see, but I questioned (to myself) how they could relegate the first love to the past so easily. However, two specific situations closer to home affected my thinking even more.

My mother was widowed at age 55, still a relatively young woman. She made a decision never to marry again and lived alone for another 38 years—longer than she had been married. I believe there were suitors, but they soon disappeared for lack of encouragement. I distinctly recall thinking her attitude was a mistake, depriving her of intimate companionship for much of her life. Now, though, I began to understand her feelings.

My father-in-law, on the other hand, was 69 when his wife died, and within a year he was seeing someone. They developed a mutually satisfying relationship that lasted until his death 30 years later. The alliance was positive for him, and I recognized its many benefits. Unfortunately, at least from my perspective, several negatives appeared in their equation, and I vowed never to accept similar ones in my own life.

Approaching the one-year anniversary of Dee's death, I remained a lonely, miserable, and somewhat depressed individual. I had adopted the practice of a walk every evening, more to pass the time than anything else. On one of those occasions, I was hailed from across the street by what I immediately observed was a good-looking woman. She identified herself as Patricia, a former volunteer at the suicide prevention center with whom I'd been paired on a crisis team over 20 years previously. We compared notes about the last decades, agreed to share a walk in the future, and parted. I somehow lost her unlisted phone number and the encounter faded from my memory.

Eventually she took it upon herself to call and we agreed to walk the next evening. We hit it off at once. The stroll encompassed more than two hours of exercise and easy conversation. We began to see each other regularly, and so began a relationship that has lasted now over seven years. A situation such as this is fraught with hurdles, some of which are still to be surmounted. I will try to describe the problems I faced. Of necessity, they will be couched in terms of my own feelings. However, it's important to recognize that your new friend may also be facing the same problems. Thus, if I have a certain need I expect my new partner to meet for me, I also have to keep in mind that I should be willing to satisfy the same need for her.

Guilt and worry accompanied this new friendship. Guilt that I was being unfaithful to Dee. Worry about what my children and friends would say.

The first was completely irrational. Certainly I wasn't being unfaithful, and Dee would have approved of emerging from self-imposed romantic exile. The only one who didn't fully understand this was me. It took awhile to admit to myself that what I was doing really was acceptable. If you're in the same situation, don't worry if you have these reservations, but also at least recognize the irrationality of the belief. In time, logic will rule and you'll be able to enjoy the pleasure of your new relationship. I was helped by the fact that Dee and I had discussed this, which is why I strongly suggest doing so while your lover is with you.

On the other hand, I think the worry about how people will react is valid. I am the most fortunate of individuals. I am blessed by family and friends who went out of their way to accept the new woman in my life. I believe it was occasionally difficult for my children, but they backed me without reservation. This was a joy for me. Patricia was particularly sensitive to the potential problems and expressed concern about others' perceptions. In spite of the obvious delight of family and friends at seeing me begin to emerge from my dark days and to look and act better, it took me a long while to become comfortable in my new role.

> *When I see gray, you show me color,*
> *When I feel despair, you offer me hope,*
> *When I embrace death, you introduce me to life.*
> *Thank you.*

I am well aware, though, that others may not be as lucky as I. It is quite possible that friends or family, particularly children, could react negatively. I am relieved I didn't have to face such a situation, but I was prepared for the eventuality. Difficult as it would have been to deal with, I had decided that this was my life and neither children nor friends could dictate the path it was to take. It's easy to say, but I know the problems are immense. If resistance had materialized, I would have explained to my children in as loving a way as possible that, just as they wanted to make their own decisions, so did I, and that I *needed* their support and love. If they refused, it would have been heartbreaking. But I would have stood my ground.

Whether the transition to a new relationship is easy or hard, it seems imperative to think of it as an *addition* to your life, not a *replacement* for part of it. You can retain the love for your past mate even as a new love emerges. Unfortunately, with Dee's father, it seemed that history was rewritten. Mention of his first wife virtually disappeared, and none of us would have dared to speak of her in the presence of the new woman. Dee, who had been extremely supportive of the new relationship, felt her mother had been abandoned, and it hurt her. I think this partially was because her father felt unnecessary guilt and reacted in the autocratic way that was typical of his defensiveness. I, on the other hand, realized I wanted to keep Dee in my life and anyone new would have to accept that. I needed to be able to continue to grieve for her, to honor anniversaries, and to be free to mention her name. And I wanted family and friends to feel similar freedom. Patricia understands this and has accepted it with amazing equanimity, even though at times it has been hard for her.

I make it a point, to this day, to assure my children that I still love their mother, and I speak of her freely. I similarly discuss Dee when I'm with friends—and with Patricia. I don't force the subject, but mention her when it is natural. I also frequently and with force tell my kids I love them. This represents no change. I always have. The key is that the new relationship has not negatively impacted my relationships with them or with their mother, and I make sure they understand that.

If there is one overriding rule to follow with a new love, I think it is *never, ever compare* her with your former mate. Don't instigate such comparisons yourself, and don't let yourself be drawn into doing so by your new friend, who may very well be feeling insecure, or by friends and family. I can't think of anything that would be more counterproductive. If you are looking for a carbon copy, you are doomed to failure. The new love is her own person, with her own history. She must be accepted for what she is, not for what you have lost. You must be attracted to her based on her own traits. She cannot be perfect, and you shouldn't expect it. And remember, your lost lover wasn't perfect either. Nor are you.

There are many practical questions that must be faced. Perhaps one of the first, if you wear a wedding ring, is whether you should remove it. For some time, I kept mine on display. It was such a part of me that I never considered any other option. Then one evening, while Patricia and I were dining out, I noticed the ring and realized I was presenting an untrue picture of a woman cavorting with a married man. It didn't seem right. My solution was to remove the ring, a not particularly simple procedure since it had welded to my expanding finger over a 42-year period. Nevertheless, with sufficient application of soap, oils, and yelps, the ring finally flew off. Then I felt naked. So I took it to a jeweler and had it enlarged slightly. For months, I would wear it much of the time and strip it off when meeting with Patricia. The percentage of time the ring adorned my finger decreased steadily until now it is only on rare occasions, when missing Dee engulfs me, that I slip it on. A recently bereaved friend wondered whether he should remove his ring. Of course, my response is the response I apply to all questions of this type: "When and only when it seems right to you." There is no correct timetable, nor does it have to happen at all.

I've already mentioned keeping pictures of Dee around my home. I have, however, reduced the quantity. And I've added a similar number of Patricia. While it is impossible here to predict all practicalities that might arise, dealing with this simple one is indicative of how I think most can be managed. Don't forget the past, but mitigate its extent. Then move equally into the future, showing your new love the same amenities you retain of your past one.

Another problem I solved employing the same philosophy was the distribution of my ashes. As mentioned previously, I had decided to have mine mixed with Dee's before final disposal of both sets. Patricia, while accepting without question the appropriateness of that action, indicated she would like some of mine to mingle with her own. It's a reasonable request, and I have left instructions to divide my ashes for the two purposes.

It is somewhat uncomfortable to discuss financial obligations, but they cannot be ignored. While Dee was outspoken about her wish for me to enter another relationship if she should die first, she was equally adamant that any family savings she had helped accumulate should either be used by me or fall to our children. I agreed readily and remain convinced that is proper. My new relationship has not yet led to marriage, but if it does we both will sign prenuptial agreements. Patricia has no interest in my money, nor I in hers, so logically this may not seem necessary. I believe, though, it is a wise move that, if nothing else, assures children you have their interests in mind. Furthermore, it eliminates what could be a messy situation in some cases. On the other hand, you also owe consideration to your new love. I think provision should be made for her in a reasonable way that is somewhat proportional to the length of time she has been with you. This suggests an increasing monetary commitment as time passes. How you work this out depends on your means and what you feel comfortable doing. Notice that what appears to me to be the proper approach again requires straddling the line between honoring the past and moving into the future.

Surely deciding whether to love again or not has to be one of the most difficult and personal decisions someone emerging from a lover's loss must face. As in so much of what I've indicated in this work, there is no best time frame. I suggest you not eliminate in your mind the possibility of finding someone new. However, it also is important that you don't rush into a new relationship.

Take the time that is right for you. Whether you choose to pursue a second love or not, life can offer you wonders that would have seemed impossible in that awful first year.

Key Points from Loving Again

- Consider at least the possibility that someday you might be interested in another love.

- On the other hand, there is no rush. You will know when the time is right.

- Realize that if new love comes, you are not being unfaithful to your first mate. Keep in mind that your lover would want you to be happy.

- Realize that whatever needs you wish your new friend to satisfy *for* you probably correspond to those she would want satisfied *by* you.

- She must accept your past life and you must accept hers, and you and she must feel free to speak of both.

- Recognize that your new love may be feeling some insecurity as she meets your family and friends.

- Understand that the new relationship is not a replacement for the old, but rather an addition appropriate for this time of your life.

- Speak honestly about your new love with your family and friends. Remember, they probably will want you to be happy. If there is dissension, try to understand it and deal with it in a loving way. However, remember it is *your* life, *your* happiness, and *your* decision.

- Assure your children and others that your love for them is unchanged, and also that you always will love your first partner.

- *Never* compare your new love with your first one, at any level.

- As problems arise, attempt to deal with them in a way that both honors the first relationship and basks in the second. Examples are keeping some of the old pictures and placing new ones, and dividing your ashes for more than one purpose.

- Remove your wedding ring when you are ready, and don't feel any rush to do so.

- Consider signing prenuptial agreements if marriage is in the offing, but also provide fairly for her.
- Keep in mind the suggestion that no major decisions be made for at least two years. There is no need to commit quickly to a new relationship.

Chapter 10

THE NEXT FEW YEARS

*Time present and time past
Are both perhaps present in time future,
And time future contained in time past.*

Four Quartets by T.S. Eliot

As I write this, it has been almost five years since I lost my Dee. What will the future hold? Of course, I can't say with any certainty. But extrapolation of current trends indicates a period of poignant memories, positive growth, professional activity, and personal enjoyment. I no longer wish to die.

Dee will be with me always. There still will be instances of intense sadness, unexpected sobs, occasional bouts of anger. A recent viewing of an ancient Ed Sullivan show provoked tears along with a fervent wish time could return to that moment when we had watched it together. The retirement we planned as a couple is taking place without her, and I feel cheated. Yes, the pain will continue at some level, and I embrace it and the associated memories.

Simultaneously, however, I am moving forward to the next phase of my life, one that includes not only memories of Dee, but also the presence of Patricia. I enjoy being with her. She is good for me. We are good for each other. The desert of my earlier existence without Dee is transforming steadily into a lush garden.

I'm sure I will call upon both Dee and Patricia during difficult times. A good friend of many years suffered a tragic accident, and the slow recovery is occurring as I write. It has been difficult for me. My labyrinth transversals now request Dee to be with him and help in his cure. Patricia, who also is his friend, accompanied me to the hospital and now participates in our frequent contacts. We encourage each other during the low periods.

With this, as with Dee's death, life goes on. And that is the message of this book.

Key Points from The Next Few Years

- Recognize it is normal to continue to experience occasional moments of grief and all its accompanying emotions.
- Look forward to the new directions in your life.
- Freely mingle the best of both the past and the present.
- Live!

PART 3

PEACE AND ADVICE

Chapter 11

Seven Years— a Snapshot

Hope springs eternal in the human breast

Pope

If your loss is recent, but you still read this chapter, you may find it difficult to give its message of hope much credence. You'll know from previous chapters that, in the past, I would have scoffed at its positive tone. Anything I say is unlikely to make you feel better, and I wouldn't attempt to convince you otherwise. So read it with doubt, recognizing that, in spite of the miseries described previously, at least in my case time has worked some of its magic.

It has been two years since I last turned to this manuscript and wrote the previous chapter, over seven years since Dee died, and well past the five-year promises to my daughter and doctor. What accounts for this time lapse? Quite simply, and poignantly, I've been busy, too busy to work on the manuscript (except for collecting rejection letters from publishers). I have been teaching some, reading a lot, doing a little traveling, polishing off some projects around the house, and building my relationship with Patricia. Life does go on, although I wouldn't have believed it seven or six or five years ago.

Much has not changed. Certainly my love for Dee is as strong as ever. My ways of honoring it continue. There still are a couple of her dresses in the closet. I still take a daily stroll through the labyrinth she created, and I write her a note in my journal every Monday (the day of the week she died) and on dates of special significance. I still "pray" for the ones she asked me to remember. I still use the electric razor she "gave" me that first Christmas after she was gone, although it probably is time for a replacement. She still presents me gifts on holidays and birthdays. And I still miss her terribly. It is definitely all right to continue to miss her and occasionally grieve, to feel tears welling, to wish things were different. But now there is more to the story.

Small and important changes have occurred. The food she made that I had kept in the freezer is gone. In spite of the admonition imparted by the medium, the fig tree withered and died under the care of my brown thumb. And the large Christmas tree is back, along with the small one that served so well during the interim years. I don't go to mediums any more, my original reservations about afterlife returning. On the other hand, I think I would visit again if a highly reputed one came along. Now, though, I think I would do it more out of curiosity than hope, although a nagging part of me would still be searching for proof.

A dreaded change is occurring. I find memories fading. I no longer see her face on passersby. I no longer expect a "visitation." Joan Didion in *The Year of Magical Thinking* said it best when speaking of her late husband, John (written one year after his death): "My sense of John himself, John alive, will become more remote, even 'mudgy,' softened, transmuted into whatever best serves my life without him. In fact, this is already beginning to happen." I don't want it to happen. But it is. I don't think I will ever come close to losing my memories, but the intensity is less and the pain of my loss appears only sporadically. In spite of all my previous admonitions, I feel some guilt about feeling better. The problem is, time, in its underhanded way, is a stronger force than one expects. And I know Dee would be pleased I'm moving on. So it does seem that, if you can survive long enough, life will improve.

And, believe it or not, improve it does. Will life ever become "normal"? How could it, when the present differs from the experiences of decades and the joint expectations for the future that were built together? Nevertheless, in some sense life *seems* normal. How can that be? Perhaps what's really happening is the definition of "normal" has changed. You and your mate had created a life that was comfortable, exciting, and sharing. It was the right life for you—*while you were a couple*. Now there are new dynamics, a new "normal." Along with everything else, your daily thoughts and activities are adapting to the new reality. This is a part of the "moving on" process. It seems to just happen, so don't be surprised.

So what is the new normality? Everyone's story is unique. This is mine. Three years ago, a triad of hurricanes hit Orlando. The third tore the roof off Patricia's apartment complex and she had only hours to extricate not only herself, but also all her possessions. She moved in with me, and all she owned was stored in a room of my house.

It has been a difficult adjustment for both of us. Patricia, used to being completely independent, had to relearn the intricacies of joint living. I, who also had been on my own for five years, had similar problems. However, it was harder for Patricia. She was faced with the fact that it is my home, and formerly Dee's home. Furthermore, I was and am unwilling to leave it to start a new home that is jointly ours. There are many reasons for this. Suffice it to say it's important to me, and I have been open about that from the beginning. So we had a real problem to solve.

We attacked it in various ways. Three of the upstairs bedrooms were turned over to Patricia. Most of "my" furniture was removed, replaced by hers. She now has a bedroom, a den, and an office. I built bookshelves in the den for her many volumes. It gives her a feeling of her own space. Unfortunately, it also leaves the house without a guest room. Patricia, trouper that she is, simply gives up one of the rooms when company arrives.

I also am making other adjustments. We plan to redo the kitchen and the laundry room. Some old art is replaced with new. Perhaps no solution is ideal, but it is beginning to work. It takes compromise that involves difficult and sometimes painful decisions. It is the practical side of blending the old and new into a modified life.

I think Patricia's moving in has been hard on my daughter, seeing a woman here who isn't her mother. But she, too, is willing to compromise, because she wants me to be happy. And I believe, by hard work on both their parts, she and Patricia are forging an even closer relationship. I have been fortunate here. I realize some family members can make it difficult for the survivor. Try to understand their concerns and explain to them how the new situation is best for you. But please remember, if there seems to be no accommodation, it is *your* life.

In a salute to our belief in a future, we have adopted three rescued greyhounds. This only after Patti urged getting a dog and I finally agreed to a single small one. But a visit to a local pet store hosting a greyhound adoption agency resulted in us both being smitten. I recognize it's a commitment, so I'd better plan on having a life for 10 more years. You never know, of course, but at least now I *want* to continue.

So, more so than any earlier time after your loss, life continues and it can be good. It won't be the same as your past or your old dreams. But it will be yours, and precious because of that.

Key Points from Seven Years—a Snapshot

- If this chapter is being read while your loss is recent, look upon it as one person's testimonial to the healing effects of time. Don't be surprised if you don't believe things can get better, but don't rule out the possibility.

- Even after seven years, or 10, or 20, it is normal to feel the loss, to continue to miss your old love, and to grieve occasionally.

- Memories do fade. This is natural. It does not mean you are being disloyal to your lover, nor should you feel any guilt.

- What was normal for you before is not necessarily so now. A new normal takes over. And that in itself is normal.

- If you share a home with a new partner, and the home originally belonged to one of you, realize it will be difficult. Both must work hard to adjust. This probably is the ultimate challenge in employing the technique of melding the old with the new.

- Recognize that living with a new partner may be hard on your family members. Be understanding of their discomfort. But remember, it is *your* life.

- Believe in the future, and that it can be good. Don't be afraid to begin new ventures.

Chapter 12

WHEN A FRIEND DIES

When someone we care about is dying, we throw out our emotional tentacles to try to pull him or her back.

Making Friends with Death by Judith L. Lief

Talking and eloquence are not the same: to speak, and to speak well, are two things.

Ben Jonson

Never does one feel oneself so utterly helpless
as in trying to speak comfort for great bereavement.

Letter to Thomas Carlyle
from his wife, Jane Welsh Carlyle

I debated the wisdom of including this chapter. I know it often is difficult for friends and even relatives to find the right words for someone who is grieving. I continue to be unsure myself, despite my own experience and despite my seeming willingness to express opinions on these pages. Other sources, including the previously mentioned books by Judith Lief and Harold Kushner, have managed to speak eloquently on this subject. I believe, however, that some of my points also might prove helpful.

One caveat: I speak below of how you can help, and it includes the suggestion to spend some time with your friend. While in general this is a good idea, always keep in mind that the ill can become tired, or may just want private time. Be alert to this and look for clues about when you should leave.

As I've stated throughout this work, there is nothing sacrosanct about my suggestions. They arise, after all, from observation of my own reactions to expressions of various types of sympathy. Another person may well respond positively to an approach that caused me to shudder. If the reader is sensitive and truly understands the grieving individual, he will find the right words without benefit of the thoughts given here.

During the trying time of illness, before death occurs, both partners need support from concerned friends. Certainly the one afflicted requires all the assistance that can be mustered. At the same time, though, the partner needs help, and that need will continue long after the death. I don't know which is the harder for most of us to deal with, the dying or the grieving. I am far from an expert, my own familiarity of association with the dying being rather limited. Mercifully, Dee's illness, or at least our knowledge of it, was short in duration— only four months. About three years ago, a good friend died after a multi-year battle with cancer, and 12 months later another succumbed to the same disease more than a decade following the diagnosis. Any thoughts I express are based mainly on these three experiences.

Few of us can imagine what someone given a terminal prognosis is feeling. This seemingly obvious observation, though, often is ignored as we frequently feed some personal need by expressing what we "know" is best for our friend. In truth, though, it is especially difficult to find the correct words, a difficulty enhanced by the ill individual's own reaction and emotional make-up. My three situations all involved people who faced their illnesses head on, accepting the diagnosis and then fighting the disease with all techniques at their disposal. Dee didn't allow anyone to call her "sick." One friend took out his frustrations with legitimate complaints about the medical profession that on more than one occasion got in the way of his best interests, and the other achieved a level of spirituality that grew continuously throughout years of remission and even during the final assault. All openly discussed their situation. Others I have known on a less intimate basis, however, have denied their illness or wanted to keep it private. Some gave up all medical intervention and turned to alternative programs in Mexico, Germany, or other parts of the globe.

Some of our friend's decisions might seem so ill-advised (at least to us) that we just *have* to say something. So how should we react? Painful as it may be, it seems to me that all we can do is keep quiet and accept her decisions, and be there to support them. This is extremely difficult when you disagree with them. But you can help most simply by listening, without prejudice. Don't force discussion. However, if your advice is requested (and it's more likely to be if you haven't tried to impose it), try to offer your views as suggestions rather than directives. And if your thoughts are rebuffed, please don't interpret this as a rejection of you. Your presence is still important, perhaps essential, to her.

I suppose, if you truly are concerned about a contemplated course of action and your opinion isn't asked, it would be acceptable, *once and once only*, to broach an alternative. After all, your friend already has been *told* what to do by doctors and others. But if you're determined to go ahead, attempt to phrase your thoughts in non-directive terms. Wording that begins something like, "I understand and respect where you're coming from. Because I care about you so much, I've been thinking about it, too, and I was wondering if you'd considered ..." is not threatening and probably has a greater chance of overcoming any resistance than any sort of imperative statement. It also indicates both your concern and your recognition that your friend is the one making the decisions.

Really, though, as a friend, your job is not to direct her course of action. Probably the most important thing you can do is keep her in your life, socializing with her in the same way you used to, doing odd, helpful jobs such as shopping, and letting her talk about the disease whenever she wishes. This can be extremely uncomfortable for you, because we don't get much training about discussing death. I think this largely is because of our own fears on the subject. I have found, however, that my experiences at being both the lover and the concerned friend have reduced my own fears, so your simple act of friendship may also be an indirect present to yourself. By the way, treating the spouse in the same way is also helpful to him. And if he is overwhelmed by his caregiver role, spelling him for a few hours would be a priceless gift.

At some point, she won't be able to continue as before. Activities will have to be curtailed, and eventually she will take to her bed for the last time. She may remain there for hours, days, weeks, or months. Don't be so afraid of losing her that you insist she get second and third opinions, that she try some new treatment about which you've read and know it is just the thing for her, that she not give up because so many depend on her. Or even worse, don't abandon her because it's too difficult for you to be with her. Believe me, I understand how hard it is to let someone go. But by now she has concluded all the fights, is tired, and has begun to make peace with the situation. She needs your love, your understanding, and your presence; even your approval and acceptance of the circumstances. If she wants your words, she'll ask for them. Often your silence is all that is necessary. Read the books by Judith Lief and Elizabeth Kübler-Ross.

The authors have had much more experience in this phase than I, and they include valuable suggestions on how to support the dying.

What I do feel qualified to discuss is how to deal with the lover who remains after the death. With few exceptions, *any* expression of sympathy is better than *no* expression of sympathy. So if you truly are concerned about the survivor and you want to show your support, the caring feelings usually will be evident in spite of any poorly chosen words. The recipient of your sympathy will understand the true intent of your message, even if the way you express it is not what you (or he) would have wished. Therefore, never forgo an opportunity to make your feelings known. The Kushner book helps with understanding this, as well as providing excellent suggestions on what to say.

So what are the "right" words? Again, that depends on the individual. However, I think there are "safe" words that have the additional advantage of being helpful.

It can never hurt to say, in whatever way is natural to you, "I'm thinking of you. Please let me know if there's anything I can do." Of course, don't say this if you don't mean it. What if you're asked for help and are unwilling?

In the same vein are phrases such as, "If you ever want to talk about her, I'd love to listen." I know I always wanted to speak of my lover. Still do for that matter. But I realize others aren't exactly waiting in line for me to do so, so I restrict comments to the special few with whom I feel comfortable. And even with them I limit the frequency. Nowadays, of course, it seems to be less and less a necessity. As with any offer to help, please don't indicate you are willing to listen unless you truly are. Remember, the grieving spouse may latch onto you for a while. However, if you are able to make such a promise, you will be providing an outlet that will be forever cherished. On the other hand, if you've made the commitment, you still have the right to be unavailable, and should feel free to state if a particular time is bad. But then indicate when would be a good time.

Furthermore, you should be sensitive to the possibility of becoming a crutch. If your friend's dependence seems to last unreasonably long, or his depression appears to be uncommonly deep, you probably should extricate yourself and lovingly suggest he seek counseling of some sort. You are not a therapist, and should never contemplate playing such a role. And, besides, you have your own life to live.

Whether by offering or not, if you find yourself acting as a listener, this means being a listener. Don't interrupt with your own concerns, which are of no interest to the grieving party at this point. Don't attempt to give advice. Don't explain how everything will be all right. Just listen, remembering that this may very well be the most painful moment your friend has ever experienced, and by listening you may be doing what is more helpful for him than anything else.

More often than not, when faced with attempting to comfort a friend, you won't be willing to make the time commitment required above. This is entirely reasonable and you should suffer no guilt. But what can you say if this is the case? I found phrases along the lines of "I'm so sorry," "I'll be thinking of you," and "I'll pray for you and her" to be helpful.

At a seminar I attended for those grieving, we were asked to construct a license plate. A lovely woman who had lost her husband created "WWJD" (What Would Jesus Do). I thought with envy that her strong faith would help her through this trying time. I suspect she responded well to expressions of sympathy based on her religious beliefs, and those who knew her would be correct to appeal to them.

I, however, have always been burdened with a questioning mind and found such comments difficult to accept. Even truly religious individuals often have trouble at this time with the inane phrases many utter. I understand they are intended to comfort, but they don't. Here are a few examples. What I thought when I heard them is shown in italics, and what I said aloud is given in boldface. "God loves you and will help you." *Sure—then why didn't He/She/It let Dee live.* **Thank you. I appreciate the thought.** "There always is a reason even though we may not understand it." *That's the biggest bunch of crap I've ever heard.* **Thank you. I appreciate the thought.** "We cannot understand God's plan for us." *Oh, please.* **Thank you. I appreciate the thought.** My verbal responses are the truth. I did appreciate the thought. Or at least the thought behind the stated thought. These good-hearted people really did want to comfort, and for that I will always be grateful. Other wonderful individuals sent me religious tracts and books, all of which were set aside and eventually discarded. Again, the thought truly is what counts. But a simple "I'm sorry" would have been so much more effective and meaningful.

I have great respect for those who find solace in their religion. But please, unless you know the grieving individual well enough to be absolutely sure how he will react to your comments, don't impose your own belief system on him, no matter how wonderful you know it to be.

Contrast the above with this alternative approach, taken by a deeply religious couple who also respect my individuality. They never felt a need to cloak their love for Dee and grief at my loss in terms of their own religious doctrine. Instead they asked for a photograph of Dee. They offered no reason and I didn't press them.

A couple of months later, they invited me to dinner at a local French restaurant. At some point in the evening, they presented me with a beautiful double-sided picture frame. One half contains the photograph I'd given them. In the other, lovingly hand-lettered, is the following well-known verse by Henri Scott Holland (1847-1919), Canon of St. Paul's Cathedral.

Death Is Nothing At All

I have only slipped away into the next room.
I am I, and you are you.
Whatever we were to each other, that we still are.
Call me by my old familiar name,
Speak to me in the easy way you always used.
Put no difference in your tone, wear no forced air of
    solemnity or sorrow.
Laugh as we always laughed at the little jokes we
    enjoyed together.
Let my name be ever the household word that it
    always was,
Let it be spoken without effect, without the trace of a
    shadow on it.
Life means all that it ever meant.
It is the same as it ever was; there is unbroken
    continuity.
Why should I be out of mind because I am out of
    sight?
I am waiting for you, for an interval.
Somewhere very near, just around the corner.
All is well.

I cannot read this without tears. The frame sits on one side of my desk, while a picture of Patricia adorns the other. This sensitive act by caring people has provided enduring comfort. If there is something similar you can do, it will undoubtedly be a source of lasting solace.

Remember that family and friends abound until the funeral or memorial service. It is later that the days become truly lonely. Ask your friend to dinner, or to a movie, or to join you in a walk. If you are refused, don't take it personally. Repeat the invitation a week later, and the week after that, and for as long as you think is reasonable. If he was a part of your group, assume he will continue to be, even if the group previously was couples only. Make it clear he is still very much wanted.

However, please want him for his own sake. Do not feel any requirement to find him a new "mate." Very dear friends had extra tickets to the opera and invited me to join them. They also invited a woman friend. I suspect there was no ulterior motive. They were merely being kind to two people special to them. But I did wonder if there was some mild hope we would get together. Maybe we would have at some later point. She is a delightful and talented woman. But it was just too early. I was at the point where I couldn't imagine being with anyone other than Dee, or ever wanting to be.

Later on, a colleague did it right. She told me she had a friend whom she thought I might enjoy, but she wasn't sure I was ready for anything like that yet. She didn't attempt to arrange a party where we were "accidentally" placed side by side. She recognized the possibility that this was not what I wanted. By this time I was seeing Patricia, so I declined. But I think with fondness about my friend who respected my feelings and let *me* make the decision.

Furthermore, if you are of the appropriate gender, don't "throw" yourself at him. One woman approached me just a few weeks after Dee's death and said, "Women are going to be letting you know they are available now. Because of that, I feel I must let you say whatever needs to be said. Do you understand what I mean?" The answer to that was simple. I didn't have a clue! At least not at the time. Later, I wondered if she was trying to indicate some interest on her part. I'm not sure of this. What I am sure of is that it was way too early to consider such a thing, and attempts to bring up "dating" (do you still call it that when you're in your 60s?) are inappropriate.

On the other hand, if your bereaved friend tells you he has found someone new, give him your wholehearted support. He'll be worried about what you think, so assure him it's great—and mean it.

In conclusion, let me re-emphasize that you shouldn't avoid contacting the bereaved because you aren't sure what to say. A few people have told me they did exactly that in my case. I understand, of course, but I would have preferred they let me know they were sorry, even if the manner in which they expressed it was not the best. Remember, if you truly care, the feelings will override the words.

Key Points from When a Friend Dies

- **During the illness, listen, listen, listen to your friends (the one who is ill *and* her mate).**

- If you are asked to make recommendations or you feel you absolutely have to even if not asked, phrase them in the form of suggestions, and be understanding if they are rejected.

- Keep socializing with your friends.

- Try to become comfortable when your friend speaks of her approaching death.

- Give the caregiver an occasional break.

- When the end is near, accept it and don't attempt to force additional opinions or alternative therapies on her. Give her your approval.

- After the death, *any* words are better than *no* words. If you know the person well, the words will be instinctively right. But even if they're not, the thought behind them will be.

- If you're willing to commit to long-range support, helpful phrases are "Is there anything I can do?" And "Do you want to talk about her?" But don't let yourself become a crutch or pseudotherapist.

- If your situation requires a lesser commitment, good comments are a heartfelt "I'm so sorry," "I'll be thinking of you," or "I'll pray for you and her."

- If you find yourself in the role of listener, do just that without turning the conversation in other directions (including about yourself) or giving advice.

- Don't impose your own belief system on the assumption it is right for your friend.

- Try to find something special and meaningful you can do that provides continuing solace.

- Include your friend in activities after the funeral or memorial service is over.

- If you have a potentially romantic interest in your friend, don't throw yourself at him. Give him time.

- Don't create situations where the goal is to establish a meeting between your friend and someone you think would be perfect for him.

- If you know of someone you think your friend might enjoy, tell him about her and let him decide if he is ready to take this big step back into life.

- If your friend announces he has been seeing someone, be enthusiastic and supportive. Make him understand you think it is wonderful.
- Remember, good friends are rare and deeply appreciated. If the grieving mate is important to you, and you handle it right, your friendship will be forever cherished.

Books Mentioned

- *Caring for the Dead: Your Final Act of Love*, Lisa Carlson, Upper Access, 1998
- *Don't Sweat the Small Stuff—and it's all small stuff*, Richard Carlson, Hyperion, 1997
- *The Year of Magical Thinking*, Joan Didion, Alfred A. Knopf, 2005
- *Hello from Heaven!: A New Field of Research—After-Death Communication—Confirms that Life and Love Are Eternal*, Bill Guggenheim and Judy Guggenheim, Bantam,1997
- *On Life After Death*, Elisabeth Kübler-Ross, PhD, Celestial Arts, 1991, 2008
- *When Bad Things Happen to Good People*, Harold S. Kushner, Anchor, 2004
- *Making Friends with Death: A Buddhist Guide to Encountering Mortality*, Judith L. Lief, Shambhala, 2001
- *The Afterlife Experiments: Breakthrough Scientific Evidence of Life After Death*, Gary E. Schwartz with William L. Simon, Pocket Books, 2002

A Few Other Books

There probably are hundreds of published books dealing with recovery from the death of a loved one, and many of them focus on loss of a spouse. A very few are listed here. Each includes subjects I haven't covered, including practical advice on everyday living, and each sometimes differs in approach from what I've outlined. But this is in keeping with the theme that everyone must seek the path that is right for him or her—there is no single correct way. From these books, from mine, and from others you can choose what seems best for you. What all the ones presented here share with mine are authors who have lost their lovers and the promise that life goes on and can become good. These references are only a few of the many fine books available in bookstores and libraries. You will notice that most are aimed specifically at widows (or females in loving relationships) while one is intended for widowers (or males in loving relationships). Certainly much of such a book applies only to the implied gender, but parts of each have general applicability and as such are useful to the other.

- *Being a Widow,* Lynn Caine, Penguin Books, 1990
- *The Widow's Handbook: A Guide for Living,* Charlotte Foehner and Carol Cozart, Fulcrum, 1988
- *Suddenly Alone: A Woman's Guide to Widowhood, Divorce and Loneliness,* Philomene Gates, Gridiron Publishers, 1999
- *Widow's Walk: One Woman's Spiritual and Emotional Journey to a New Life,* Anne Hosansky, iUniverse, 2000
- *The Widower,* Jane Burgess Kohn and Willard K. Kohn, Beacon Press, Boston, 1978 (a large though dated bibliography is included)

Appendix

My Comments at Dee's Memorial August 26, 1999

I want to welcome you to what I hope will be a joyful celebration of a wonderful woman's life. I hope my words, and those of others, will help us all understand better this complicated, giving individual who contributed so much to her world.

Does it surprise anyone here that Dee was very clear about what she wanted today? Or does it surprise anyone that her biggest concern was for those of us left behind? She wants this to be a spiritual uplifting during which we treasure those moments we were lucky enough to have with her. And during which we remember with elation how she has touched our lives, and how she will continue to as we face the future, combining our own inherent humanity with the wisdom she has shared with us. She assured me that she has entered a small place in every cell of each of our bodies, and that we can count on her whenever we need help. I'm depending on that.

There is no adequate way to describe the incredible journey of love and sharing the two of us have taken these past 42 years. But I can certainly proclaim how proud I am of the life choices she made. She spent the first half of her existence learning the basics of what would become her life's mission: art, music, philosophy, religion, teaching, writing, caring, loving, understanding. And raising two extraordinary children of whom she was exceptionally proud. It was only natural that she become a therapist, spending 12 years at Orlando Regional Medical Center, where she initiated innovative mind/body programs. It was here she learned how to fight the establishment in order to introduce her "radical" ideas.

And then came the incredible Getting Well experience. I have watched in awe as she again challenged conventional wisdom to create, by the force of her vision and strength alone, the positive environment for healing that eventually located at this lovely campus. I stared with disbelief as people with so-called terminal or life-inhibiting physical problems overcame them and often bid them goodbye. I finally came to understand though, after much instruction from Dee, that, wonderful as such recoveries were, they were not the ultimate goal, the very essence of healing, which is living whatever time we have been given with grace and joy. She set a pretty good example, didn't she? I burst with pride as I saw her offer her program to anyone who truly wanted it, independent of ability to pay. I beamed with pleasure when I'd think of the comfort her acclaimed book has brought to thousands throughout the world. And I've come to love all of you whom I've met through the program, as well as those of you who have crossed my life via other paths.

There was a pope, I think it was Pope John II but I could be wrong, who, near death, responded to his many faithful followers praying for his recovery by saying, "There are no miracles for popes." I was tempted to close by asserting there are no miracles for directors of mind/body programs. But it's not true. Look around you. Every one of you has been touched directly or indirectly in some way by Dee, creating never-ending miracles that will live on in you and be passed on to others.

Thank you for coming. As we remember Dee today, laugh a lot (remember her sly and wicked sense of humor), cry if you want (remember how she always wanted us to be in touch with our feelings), and fully live the moment. Above all, let's attempt to gain strength from the lesson she taught and, up until her last hour, was still struggling to master herself: Learn to accept gracefully what the universe presents rather than demanding the universe present what we want.

Thank you.

About the Author

Robert C. Brigham is Professor Emeritus of Mathematics at the University of Central Florida. He teaches the occasional course, tutors, and is an active participant in two research groups.

He was employed as an engineer for 12 years, the last seven at Bell Telephone Laboratories where he was involved in the development of the telephone company's first electronic switching system. Upon attaining his doctorate in 1970 from New York University, he moved with his wife, Deirdre, to her home of Orlando, Florida and embarked on a 33-year life in academia. He has won awards for excellence in both teaching and research.

Deirdre was a counselor who designed and founded a behavioral medicine program for those with life-threatening and life-challenging diseases, 10 years before these techniques became common components of many hospital programs.

After 42 years of marriage, Deirdre was diagnosed with lung cancer and succumbed to it just four months later, shortly more than a year after the death of both her father and her sister from the same disease. Deirdre's passing was a devastating experience for the author, and motivated him to examine his recovery, and then write about his experiences and share his insights in this book.

Dr. Brigham continues to live in Orlando and, in addition to his mathematics, works in his shop, loves and cares for his three rescued greyhounds, and shares his life with Patricia, his companion of seven years.

978-0-595-48633-5
0-595-48633-9